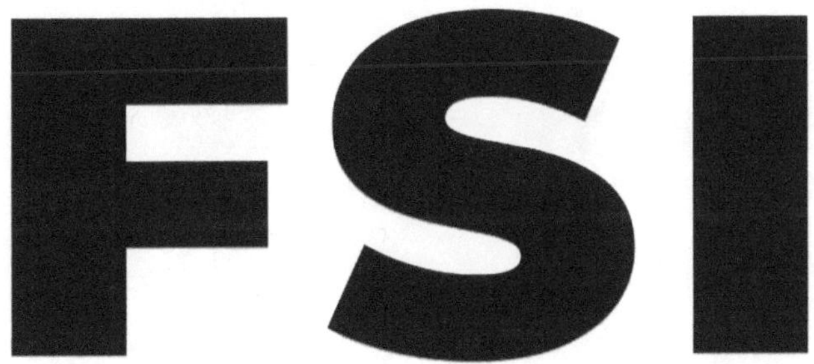

AF442511

Adv. DARSH DHAROD
Dr. Adv. HARSHUL SAVLA

INDIA · SINGAPORE · MALAYSIA

ISBN 979-8-89186-398-9

Index

About the Author

Adv. Darsh Rekha Ketan Dharod

Adv. Darsh Rekha Ketan Dharod is a young millennial of 27 years having keen interest and plethora of knowledge about the Real Estate Industry.

Adv. Darsh has been keenly watching and tracking the real estate industry from about when he was in his pre-teens, the spark and interest kicked-off in him while visiting a few under construction projects and subsequent interactions with key stakeholders and stalwarts from the industry.

Adv. Darsh is an alumnus of Bombay Scottish School, Mahim an institution which is 176 years old, ranked among the top 2 in Mumbai and top 6 in India. He stood among the top 1 percent in the country in the ICSE Board 10th Grade examinations and HSC 12th Grade examinations.

Adv. Darsh has degrees in Accountancy, Finance, Management and Law having studied Bachelors of Accountancy and Finance (B.A.F) from H.R. College of Commerce and Economics in which he stood at 6th Rank in entire University of Mumbai, Bachelors of Law (LL.B) from K.C. Law College, Masters of Commerce in Management (M.Com) from University of Mumbai, Masters of Law (LL.M) with specialization in Human Rights from University of Mumbai, and is currently in the last and final stage of completing Chartered Accountancy (CA) from Institute of Chartered Accountants of India and Chartered Financial Analyst (CFA) from CFA Institute, USA.

Adv. Darsh started working rather at an early age of 19 years while still in college, managing both studies and work which has helped him work in different industries & sectors, gain insights into each of them and build expertise across. Apart from Real Estate, he has worked in domains such as Investment Banking, Private Equity, Strategy, Consulting & Legal.

Adv. Darsh as part of Chartered Accountancy course has completed 3 years of articleship, there after worked in Tata Capital, in Special Projects developing a new digital platform enabling the dream of 'One Tata' which eventually took the shape as the super app 'Tata Neu'. He later worked at HDFC Property Ventures a Real Estate Private Equity Fund and a HDFC Group Company and IEG Investment Banking Group, a German based Investment Bank. He also worked at Colliers International in their Consulting and Advisory team, in which he advised on various Real Estate Developments and Asset classes to top Developers, Industrialists and Governments in 25 cities across 7 States and 2 UTs in India. He currently works at Adani Realty in CEOs Office- Strategic Projects looking after Dharavi Redevelopment Project which is Asia's Largest Urban Regeneration and Slum Rehabilitation Project, and similar large scale redevelopment projects.

Adv. Darsh has been recipient of many prestigious awards in his life from institutions including Governments, such as the "R.K. Sharma

Memorial Prize" for highest distinction in ICSE Examinations, Letter of Appreciation from Mr. Rajendra Darda, Editor-in-chief Lokmat and Minister of School Education in Government of Maharashtra. He was felicitated with various awards during his college years for his contribution to college and academic performance by Dr. Indu Shahani, Principal of H.R. College of Commerce and Economics and former Sheriff of Mumbai. He's also been recipient of awards by Bombay Scottish School, K.C. Law College, KVO, LNMA, PSS, MG among many others.

Adv. Darsh is actively involved and one of the youngest committee members in the history of CREDAI MCHI (Confederation of Real Estate Developers' Association of India & Maharashtra Chamber of Housing Industry), where he is a part of Statistics and Research Wing. CREDAI MCHI has more than 1800 Developers as its members across 14 City Chapters making up for entire Mumbai Metropolitan Region.

Adv. Darsh is also actively involved and is also one of the youngest committee members in the history of CREDAI National Youth Wing, where he is a part of Business Process Automation Committee. CREDAI National has more than 13,300 Developers as its members in 21 States and 230 City Chapters across India.

Adv. Darsh is also an International Best-Selling Author and has authored more than 8 books on the Real Estate Sector, making his books one of India's and possibly the World's most comprehensive literatures on Real Estate Sector. Some of his books are: Self-Redevelopment & Reviving Stalled Projects, Alternative Real Estate, Insolvency & Bankruptcy Code, Judicial Journey under RERA, ERA post RERA, Funding Options for Developers, FSI- A Development Control Tool, ESG in Real Estate Sector etc.

Adv. Darsh due to his rich and diversified academic and professional experience, regularly holds Seminars and Is also a Guest Lecturer on different topics covering Finance, Law, Real Estate, among others at prestigious colleges across India. He has also written articles and snippets for a few newspapers, magazines and journals.

Adv. Darsh has mentored over 50 students pursuing their Masters, MBA and other specialization courses from institutions and universities such as NMIMS, IIT- Kharagpur, CEPT, NICMAR, RICS, GLC, MIT, UC Berkley, Cranfield, HSNC, Nirma, KC law, Amity among others. Adv. Darsh has also been the guide for final year Dissertation, Thesis, DRP for many of the above students.

Adv. Darsh is also actively involved in a few NGOs and for his contributions to society has been facilitated by Ministry of Railways, Government of India among many other organizations. He has also represented India at an UNESCO event held in Europe and Turkey.

Adv. Darsh has keen interest in sports, has run several Marathons and been a Gold Medalist in Swimming, Chess and Badminton.

About the Author

Dr. Adv. Harshul Savla (MRICS)

Dr. Adv. Harshul Savla (MRICS) is Managing Partner of M Realty (Suvidha Lifespaces) which has successfully completed more than 2 million sq.ft. in last 34 years across Mumbai City under the able leadership of Mr. Pramesh Rambhiya. CRISIL India and Realty Icon Awards recognized Dr. Harshul as "Young Thought Leader" and Realty NXT featured him as "Young Turk of Real Estate Sector". He has won the prestigious CREDAI-MCHI Golden Pillar Award in the category of Best Debutant Real Estate Developer and has been awarded "Young Achiever of the Year" by ET NOW, CNN News 18, ZEE Business, MAHARASHTRA Times, ABP News, Realty+, MID DAY, Business World and Realty Quarter.

Dr. Harshul has featured in the Business World and Realty Plus "40 under 40" list as Real Estate's Young Turk consecutively in 2021, 2022 and 2023. He has also been awarded the prestigious "Pillars of Maharashtra" award in 2022 by Hon'ble Member of Parliament for Mumbai North. The Times Group's Economic Times has awarded Dr. Harshul Savla as an Inspiring Personality 2022 for exceptional contribution to Real Estate Sector. Mid Day's "Success Stories 2022" has featured Dr. Harshul's various achievements and journey. He has been a TEDx Speaker too.

Dr. Harshul has worked as EA to Ramesh Nair, former Chairman, JLL India and has worked in the Wealth Management Team at TATA Capital where he was awarded the National Award for Exemplary Performance. He is a perfect blend of Corporate Experience along with stellar education credentials of Ph.D., LL.M, LL.B, MBA and BMS from prestigious institutions like JBIMS, GLC, NM and Department of Law, University of Mumbai.

Dr. Harshul holds the World Record for "Maximum Degree from Single University" and his World Record is mentioned in World Book of Records London, The British World Records, International Book of Records, International Talent Book of Records, Exclusive World Record, Asian World Records, Global Records & Research Foundation, Amazing Indian Records, World Records India, India Book of Records, Kohinoor Vidyasamrat, Champion Book of World Record, High Range Book of World Records etc.

He also holds the World Record for "Maximum Books Authored & Published in a Year" for authoring and publishing 12 Real Estate Books in the year 2021 in English Language. Dr. Harshul is awarded as "Author of the Year" at the prestigious CNBC Awaaz Real Estate Excellence Awards 2022 held at Taj Lands End, Mumbai.

Dr. Harshul was awarded Doctorate (Ph.D.) for his Thesis on REITs (Real Estate Investment Trusts) which is first such thesis in India on the said subject and the Thesis is also available in the form of a book. Apart from this he is an NSE Certified Market Professional - Level 4 and has done a course on 'Strategic Real Estate Management' from ISB, Hyderabad.

Dr. Harshul is "Chairman: Statistics & Standards" at CREDAI National, which has more than 13,300 Real Estate Developers as its Members and has presence in 230 Cities (21 State Chapters). He is Research Convenor of CREDAI MCHI and heads its Statistics & Research Wing. CREDAI MCHI is a leading Real Estate Developers Association of MMR having 1,800 members across its 14 Units. Dr. Harshul has also served as the National Head of the Committee on E-Learning and Masterclass at CREDAI National Youth Wing from 2021-2023 and is presently the "Chairman: Business Process Optimization"

Dr. Harshul is also an Amazon Best Selling Author and has authored 20 books on the Real Estate Sector and General Management, making his books one of India's most comprehensive literatures on Real Estate Sector. Some of his books are: Real Estate Laws, Reality of Realty, Real Estate Valuation, Affordable Housing, NBFC & HFC Crisis, Fractional Ownership & REITs, Insolvency & Bankruptcy Code, Self-Redevelopment & Reviving Stalled Projects, Digitalizing Real Estate Sector in Built Environment, Building Information Modeling, Green Buildings, Facility Management, COVID-O-NOMICS, Luxury Retail, Alternative Real Estate, Judicial Journey under RERA, Self-Redevelopment and Reviving Stalled Projects, NCLT & IBC in Real Estate Sector, ERA POST RERA, Funding Options for Developers, FSI – A Development Control Tool etc. He regularly writes articles for fortnightly business magazine "Property House" and may other newspapers and journals.

Dr. Harshul is Associate Professor at ITM University and is also a Ph.D. Guide / Supervisor with them. He was a Visiting Faculty and Guest Lecturer at the prestigious RICS School of Built Environment, Mumbai Campus. He taught the subject 'Real Estate Development Process' to Management Students at the Mumbai Campus. He was also a Guest Lecturer at REMI - The Real Estate Management Institute, Mumbai. He was Invited to conduct Session on REITs in India for Developers Members of NAREDCO and was one of the youngest Member Developer to do so. He has also delivered a lecture at PEATA (I) on Future of Realty. He is also a renowned moderator for panels discussing various aspects of Realty and has moderated more than 60 panel discussions so far.

Dr. Harshul has recently embarked his research journey for his second Ph.D. which he is pursuing from the Department of Law, University of Mumbai under the guidance of Former HOD of the Department. His thesis is on the topic of RERA and will be the first Ph.D. in Law thesis in India on RERA.

Dr. Harshul is also the Founding Member of the "RERA Practitioners' Welfare Association" and the Founding Member of "IRIYA Realty Intelligentsia and Advisory Foundation of India" which comprises of Innovation Centre, Think Tank and Centre of Excellence. Dr. Harshul is also part of the Managing Committee of IBG (India Business Group). Dr. Harshul is a Founding Member at the 500 MBA Club and also a Mentor at the Founder Institute which is the world's most proven network to turn ideas into fundable startups and startups into global businesses.

About the Co-Author

Shanay Ketan Dharod

Meet Shanay Dharod, a remarkable young individual with an insatiable thirst for knowledge and a passion for excellence in the worlds of finance, investment, and sports. At just 23 years old, Shanay's journey has already been defined by extraordinary achievements and a drive to make a lasting impact in multiple domains.

Hailing from the esteemed Bombay Scottish School, Mahim, an institution steeped in tradition and excellence, Shanay's educational foundation laid the groundwork for his future successes. Building on this strong base, he furthered his academic pursuits, earning a bachelor's degree in Banking and Insurance from H.R. College of Commerce and Economics and a master's degree in commerce with a specialization in Advanced Accounting from R. A. Poddar College. Not content to stop there, Shanay's hunger for knowledge led him to pursue an illustrious MSc in Investment Management at the prestigious Cranfield School of Management in the United Kingdom, where he ranked 1st in the cohort.

Shanay's pursuit of excellence extends beyond the classroom, early on, he delved into the finance industry, embarking on internships at brokerage houses, wealth management firms, and equity research institutions during his undergraduate years. He started his full-time professional journey having worked at Acuité Rating & Research Limited, a Credit Rating Agency and at M Realty, a Real Estate Company. He currently works at GMEX Group (ZERO13), a trailblazing financial markets infrastructure company based in London, United Kingdom. He played a pivotal role in the groundbreaking ZERO13 initiative—a carbon credits exchange. Spearheading critical research efforts and comprehensive financial modeling skills demonstrated his acute analytical acumen.

Beyond the world of finance, Shanay is also a force to be reckoned with on the squash court. As an active participant and passionate advocate of the sport, he has achieved remarkable success, earning an All-India Rank of 39th and an All-Asia Rank of 134th in squash. As the Founder of the Cranfield Squash Society, he brings his leadership skills to the fore, fostering a community of squash enthusiasts and promoting the sport's growth.

He actively engages in philanthropic endeavors, dedicating his time to NGOs and contributing to vaccination drives for COVID-19. As a well-rounded individual with a diverse set of talents and interests, Shanay also proudly represented India at an UNESCO event held in Turkey, showcasing his cultural appreciation and global perspective.

Shanay's life has been adorned with a multitude of prestigious awards, from the Merit Award for excellence in ICSE and HSC Examinations to various college and squash-related accolades, including those from the Squash Rackets Federation of India and Asian Squash Federation. His exceptional academic performance, contributions to college life, and remarkable skills on the squash court have earned him well-deserved recognition, making him an inspiring role model for others to follow.

Shanay has contributed to a few Amazon Best Selling Books on Real Estate Sector. Some of them are: Self-Redevelopment & Reviving Stalled Projects, Insolvency & Bankruptcy Code, ERA post RERA, FSI- A Development Control Tool.

Research Team

Krish Rambhiya
B.S Industrial Engineering and Operations Research,
B.A Data Science, University of California, Berkeley

Eeshan Samangaonkar
BE. Civil from VJTI

Pooja Bhanushali
MBA (Real Estate) from NMIMS

Siddhi More
MBA (Real Estate) from NMIMS

Gaurang Bhandwalkar
MBA (Real Estate) from NMIMS

Anooj Pradhan
MBA (Real Estate) from NMIMS

Jerome Selvan

MBA (Real Estate) from NHSMRE

Zulfiquar Syed

MBA (Real Estate) from NHSMRE

Atharva Kadam

B.COM from KC College

Chapter 1

Land And Its Usage

Introduction

Land usage throughout history is an interesting story that reveals the ingenuity and evolution of human civilisations. In the ancient world, hunter-gatherer societies roamed the land for shelter. Moving from one place to another, they adapted to different terrains and climates.

As time passed, a significant shift occurred with the emergence of agriculture around 10,000 BCE. People began to settle in one place, cultivating crops and rearing livestock. Fertile lands became the backbone of settled farming communities. Ancient civilisations like the Indus Valley, Sumerians, Egyptians and Mayans developed irrigation systems to maximise agricultural productivity, relying on the land's fertility to grow crops.

The rise of empires brought forth new land uses. Ancient Greeks, Romans, and Persians established cities and constructed impressive structures. Roads and aqueducts spanned vast distances, connecting territories and facilitating trade. The land was a foundation for these great civilisations, supporting their urban centres, palaces, temples, and public buildings.

Feudalism dominated the mediaeval period in Europe, where land became the currency of power. Lords claimed vast tracts of land and bartered it in exchange for military service or labour. The land was used for agriculture and grazing livestock, sustaining a hierarchical society. Fortresses and castles stood as symbols of authority, overlooking the estates and offering protection.

The age of exploration marked a new chapter in land usage as European powers embarked on voyages to conquer and colonise distant lands. Native populations were often displaced, and the acquired lands were exploited for resources and plantation agriculture. The colonisers reshaped the landscapes to suit their needs, forever altering the relationship between people and land.

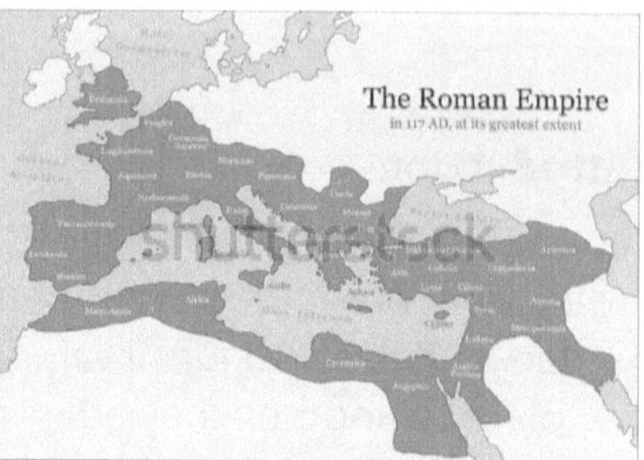

The Industrial Revolution brought profound changes as mechanisation and urbanisation took hold. Land was transformed to accommodate factories, mines, and sprawling cities. Agricultural practices became more efficient and productive, with machinery revolutionising how crops were grown and harvested. The land became a canvas for progress and development, adapting to the demands of an industrialised society.

In the modern era, i.e., the technological revolution, land usage has become increasingly diverse and specialised. Urban areas, commercial zones, industrial parks, agricultural lands, and protected natural areas coexist. The world's population continues to grow, placing greater pressure on available land and necessitating sustainable land management practices.

Land Usage Patterns in India

Land use patterns in India have changed dramatically over the ages due to variables such as population expansion, urbanisation, industrialisation, and agricultural practices. Here is a timeline of land use in India from ancient times to the present:

Ancient India - The land use pattern in ancient India was primarily agricultural. The Indus Valley Civilization had an advanced agricultural system with irrigation and ploughs. Agriculture expanded throughout the Vedic period, focusing on animal husbandry and crop production, such as wheat, barley, and rice.

Medieval India - Agriculture dominated land use patterns during the mediaeval period. Tobacco, maize, and potatoes were introduced during the Mughal Empire (1526-1857). However, the Mughal Empire's growth also resulted in deforestation and the conversion of forests to farmland.

Modern India - The commercialisation of agriculture, the establishment of the Zamindari system, forest protection regulations, land acquisition for infrastructural development, urbanisation, and industrialisation characterised land use patterns in British India.

Independent India - Following independence in 1947, India's land use pattern changed dramatically. The Green Revolution of the 1960s resulted in the introduction of high-yielding crop types and the usage of chemical fertilisers and pesticides, considerably enhancing agricultural production. The expansion of urbanisation and industrialisation led to the transfer of agricultural land for non-agricultural use.

The Liberalisation Era - The liberalisation era in India refers to a period of economic reforms and policy changes implemented in the early 1990s. During this time, the Indian government introduced measures to open up the economy, reduce government control, and promote private-sector participation. These reforms aimed to shift from a centrally planned economy to a more market-oriented system. The liberalisation era brought about changes such as the relaxation of trade barriers, the encouragement of foreign direct investment, the deregulation of industries, and the modernisation of financial systems. These reforms significantly impacted India's economic growth, global integration, and the expansion of sectors like information technology and services.

Growing Importance of FSI since the Liberalisation of India

Floor Space Index is a term used to measure the total floor area of a building in relation to the size of the land on which it is built. It is often referred to as Floor Area Ratio (FAR).

The Floor Space Index (FSI) is universally used in real estate and is a standard for controlling building height in urban areas. It is the ratio of the total built-up area to the total plot area. The higher the ratio, the bigger the building that can be built on the same amount of land.

Since the liberalisation era in India, which began in the early 1990s, FSI has gained increased importance due to several factors:

- Rapid Urbanisation: The liberalisation era brought about economic reforms and a shift towards a market-oriented economy, leading to rapid urbanisation. With the growth of cities and towns, there has been a surge in demand for housing, commercial spaces, and infrastructure. FSI has become crucial in managing this urban growth and regulating the density of construction.

- Accommodating Population Growth: The current population of India is approximately 1.42 billion and has grown significantly over the years, resulting in increased pressure on available land resources. FSI allows for higher vertical development, such as high-rise buildings, which helps accommodate the growing population within limited land areas.

- Maximising Land Utilisation: With the scarcity of land in urban areas, optimising land utilisation has become imperative. FSI regulations enable efficient use of available land by allowing developers to construct taller buildings or increase the number of units on a given plot. This helps make the most of limited land resources.

- Attracting Foreign Direct Investment (FDI): The liberalisation era in India witnessed a greater inflow of foreign direct investment (FDI) into the real estate sector. FSI regulations and policies play a significant role in attracting such investments. Developers often look for higher FSI limits to increase the potential return on investment by constructing larger and more profitable projects.

- Economic Growth and Employment Generation: India is a USD 3.7 trillion economy in 2023, i.e., now the fifth largest economy in the world, and is estimated to be a USD 10 trillion economy by 2035. The real estate and construction sectors contribute significantly to India's GDP and employment generation. The liberalisation era brought about increased private sector participation in real estate development. FSI regulations, when implemented effectively, provide clarity and transparency, making it easier for developers to plan and execute projects, leading to economic growth and job creation.

- Infrastructural Development: FSI regulations have become crucial in infrastructure development. With urbanisation, there is a need to align the FSI limits with the capacity of existing infrastructure, including transportation networks, water supply, sewage systems, and public amenities. FSI regulations help ensure that the available infrastructure adequately supports the built environment.

- Affordable Housing and Redevelopment: FSI regulations have also gained importance in the context of affordable housing and redevelopment projects. Authorities may provide additional FSI or incentives to promote the construction of affordable housing units or to encourage the redevelopment of dilapidated or underutilised areas, contributing to urban renewal and inclusive growth.

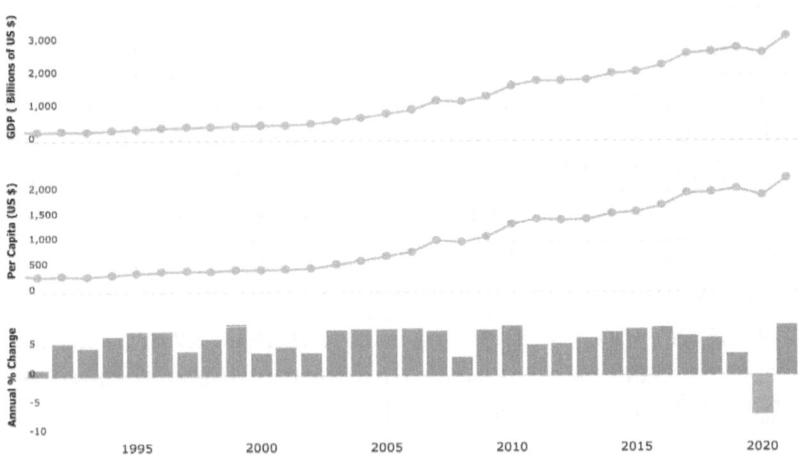

(Fig: GDP Growth of India from 1991 to 2023)

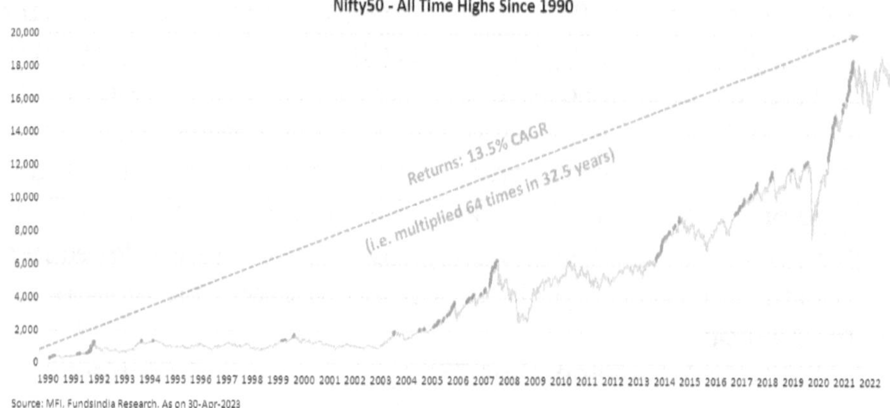

(Fig: NIFTY 50 index)

Summary

The evolution of land has been a dynamic process since its existence. There have been many advancements, and many more are expected to happen exponentially. The evolution of civilisations has been inextricably related to the utilisation of land throughout history. Agricultural civilisations were distinguished by crop cultivation and the construction of irrigation systems, which enabled agricultural expansion and population growth. With the rise of large-scale companies and the transfer of agricultural land to industrial land, the Industrial Revolution resulted in considerable changes in land use patterns. The late-twentieth-century Technological Revolution resulted in the adoption of new agricultural technologies and the creation of smart cities, leading to the modification of land use patterns. These historical events have had far-reaching consequences for the economy, society, and environment, influencing how humans interact with and use land resources. Acknowledging the historical background of land use patterns and aiming towards sustainable practices that balance economic development, social fairness, and environmental conservation is critical.

Chapter 2

FSI: Residential

FSI Regulations in India

Let us look at the FSI rules and regulations for residential properties in the top cities in India.

Mumbai

Width of the road (in metres)	Island	Suburbs
Under 9m	1.33	1
9-12 m	2	2
12-18 m	2.4	2.2
18-27 m	2.7	2.4
27 m and above	3	2.5

Pune

Width of the road (in metres)	Minimum size of the plot (in sq m)	Permissible maximum FSI
9-12 m	Below 1,000	2
12-18 m	Above 1,000	2.5
18-24 m	Above 2,000	3
24-30 m	Above 3,000	3.5
30 m and above	Above 4,000	4

Hyderabad

Hyderabad is the only city in India with no limit on the FSI value, with an average hovering from 6 to 7, whereas the Indian national average FSI ranges between 2 to 2.5.

Ahmedabad

FSI in Ahmedabad's prime localities is 1.2, which extends up to 1.8 for certain localities towards the suburbs. The base FSI is 1.8 for the R1 Zone and 1.2 for the R2 Zone in Ahmedabad. A developer can buy extra FSI up to 4 depending on the width of the road. Chargeable FSI is the largest share of non-tax revenue income for the Ahmedabad Municipal Corporation.

Bengaluru

Bengaluru has three types of localities – Intensely Developed localities, Moderately Developed localities, and Sparsely developed localities. Depending on this category, plot size, and road width, the FSI can vary between 1.75 to 3.35.

Delhi

Delhi has not imposed FSI on group housing. According to the Delhi Master Plan 2021, the FSI ranges between 1.2 to 3.5. The governing body allows more FSI for plots that have a direct impact due to the Delhi metro. Redevelopment projects have FSI of 4.

Analysis of FSI policies in Indian cities

FSI policies in different cities in India exhibit a diverse range of approaches and regulations to manage residential development. However, a critical examination of these policies reveals several shortcomings and areas for improvement.

Mumbai: In Mumbai, the FSI policy aims to address the challenges of population density and slum rehabilitation. While the intention is commendable, the implementation often needs more transparency. The policy's focus on increasing vertical growth and redeveloping slums has led to overcrowding, strain on infrastructure, and inadequate provision of essential amenities in many areas. Even the Slum Rehabilitation Scheme which was launched decades ago has failed to address the problems of slums in Mumbai with hardly a certain percentage getting rehabilitation while majority still continue to stay in slums

Delhi: Delhi's zonal-based FSI policy appears logical in theory, aiming to balance development and infrastructure capacity. However, the lack of proper enforcement and monitoring mechanisms has resulted in widespread violations and unauthorised constructions. The zoning classifications often need to consider the ground realities, resulting in uneven development and neglect of infrastructure requirements in certain areas.

Bengaluru: Bengaluru's revised FSI policy promotes affordable housing and sustainable practices. However, the implementation has been inconsistent, with limited incentives for developers to comply. The policy's focus on integrating public amenities and open spaces within residential projects is often disregarded, leading to a lack of proper community infrastructure and inadequate green spaces.

Chennai: Chennai's FSI policy, emphasising mitigating natural disasters, is commendable. However, the effectiveness of the policy is questionable, as it does not address the main causes of vulnerability, such as encroachments and inadequate stormwater drainage systems. The lower FSI limits in vulnerable areas do little to prevent unauthorised constructions, leaving residents at risk during natural calamities.

Kolkata: The focus on preserving heritage structures through lower FSI limits is appreciable in Kolkata. However, the policy needs to balance keeping and accommodating the growing population. The stringent regulations often hinder the development of modern and sustainable housing options, increasing pressure on the limited available space.

Pune: Pune's FSI policy, which incentivises sustainable practices and affordable housing, holds promise. However, the lack of proper enforcement and monitoring has resulted in developers bypassing these requirements and prioritising profit over sustainable and affordable development. The policy's provisions for open spaces and amenities often remain on paper, depriving residents of much-needed recreational areas.

Ahmedabad: Ahmedabad's Development Control Regulation (DCR) attempts to balance development, heritage preservation, and environmental considerations. However, the policy's implementation needs consistent enforcement and clarity. The adaptive reuse of heritage structures often needs to be addressed, and the provision of open spaces and amenities within residential developments is frequently overlooked.

In conclusion, while FSI policies in different cities in India demonstrate an intent to address urban development challenges, they are plagued by inadequate enforcement, inconsistent implementation, and a lack of transparency. These shortcomings have resulted in haphazard growth, strain on infrastructure, and neglect of essential amenities. To improve the effectiveness of FSI policies, there is a need for stronger enforcement mechanisms, better coordination between various agencies, and a focus on sustainable and inclusive development that meets the needs of the growing urban population.

General Overview of the FSI Policies in international cities

City	Country	Residential Development Policy	Aim of their FSI policy
Tokyo	Japan	Encourages high-rise residential development and mixed-use zoning	Emphasis on earthquake-resistant construction, efficient land use, and accommodating population growth
New York City	United States	Allows for a mix of high-rise, mid-rise, and low-rise residential developments	Zoning regulations vary by neighbourhood and encourage affordable housing, contextual design, and open spaces.
Singapore	Singapore	Implements strict planning controls and guidelines for residential developments	Focuses on ensuring a mix of public and private housing, sustainable design, and promoting social integration

City	Country	Residential Development Policy	Aim of their FSI policy
London	United Kingdom	Emphasises mixed-use developments and urban regeneration	Encourages a mix of housing types, affordable housing provision, sustainable design, and community facilities
Berlin	Germany	Promotes diverse and affordable housing options with strict rent control	Prioritises social housing, cooperative models, and maintaining affordable rental rates
Sydney	Australia	Focuses on urban infill and medium-density residential development	Balances housing supply and demand, promote sustainable design, and preserves green spaces
Dubai	United Arab Emirates	Facilitates high-rise luxury residential developments	Emphasis on luxury and high-end residential projects, often catering to the international market
Shanghai	China	Implements controlled urban growth with a mix of high-rise and mid-rise housing.	Focuses on balancing population density, promoting sustainable development, and providing adequate amenities
Paris	France	Implements strict regulations to preserve historic character and aesthetics	Emphasis on maintaining architectural heritage, protecting historic neighbourhoods, and preserving urban form

Learnings to take from global FSI policies

One of the strengths observed in several global FSI policies is the emphasis on **sustainability**. Singapore and Sydney have incorporated sustainable design principles, energy efficiency measures, and green building practices into their FSI regulations. These practices reduce environmental impact, enhance resource efficiency, and promote a healthier living environment. Indian cities can learn from these examples and integrate sustainability considerations into their FSI policies, encouraging developers to adopt eco-friendly practices and promoting green infrastructure.

Another area of opportunity is **affordability**. Some cities, including Berlin and New York City, have implemented measures to address housing affordability through FSI policies. These include rent control regulations, affordable housing quotas, and incentives for providing affordable units. Indian cities grappling with housing affordability challenges can explore similar strategies to ensure that FSI policies contribute to creating affordable housing options for various income groups.

Community engagement is a crucial aspect that can be strengthened in FSI policies. Cities like London and Paris have incorporated provisions for public amenities, open spaces, and community facilities within residential developments, fostering community cohesion and enhancing the quality of life for residents. Indian cities can leverage FSI policies to ensure the provision of such amenities, encouraging community participation in decision-making processes and creating vibrant and inclusive neighbourhoods.

Design quality is another important consideration. Cities like Tokyo and Dubai have implemented regulations to ensure high-quality architecture and construction practices. These policies prioritise earthquake-resistant structures, contextual design, and aesthetic considerations. Indian cities can adopt similar design guidelines within their FSI policies to promote visually appealing and culturally sensitive residential developments contributing to the overall urban fabric.

Furthermore, the comparative analysis highlights the importance of tailoring global best practices to local conditions. Indian cities have unique challenges and opportunities, such as high population densities, cultural diversity, and varying levels of infrastructure development. By adapting successful elements from global examples and considering local context, Indian cities can enhance their FSI policies to address specific needs and aspirations.

Chapter 3

FSI: Commercial

Commercial Real Estate

If real estate is used for making money, is rented out for investments, or falls into several other categories other than being a private residence, it is considered commercial real estate.

Commercial properties, also called as investment or income properties, refers to buildings or land used for generating profit through rental income or capital gain.

Below is a list of commercial real estate that you see everyday:

- Office buildings
- Apartment buildings great than five units
- Retail shopping centres
- Medical offices
- Self-storage facilities
- Industrial complexes
- Warehouses
- Mobile home parks
- Hotels, resorts, and so on

FSI Regulations for Commercial Real Estate in India's top cities

Mumbai: The FSI norms for a commercial Real Estate asset in Mumbai as per DCPR 2034 published by Mumbai Municipal Corporation's Town Planning Department are as shown below:

FSI FOR OFFICE SPACE DEVELOPMENT IN THE ISLAND CITY			
Road width	TOTAL FSI		DIFFERENCE
	Prior to DCPR 2034	As per DCPR 2034	
> 12m	2.30	4.05	1.76
> 18m	2.57	5.40	2.84
> 27m	2.70	6.75	4.05

Source: Knight Frank Research, DCPR 2034

FSI FOR OFFICE SPACE DEVELOPMENT IN SUBURBS			
Road width	TOTAL FSI		DIFFERENCE
	Earlier	Now	
> 12m	2.97	4.05	1.08
> 18m	3.24	5.40	2.16
> 27m	3.375	6.75	3.375

Source: Knight Frank Research, DCPR 2034

Mumbai's rental rates differ from those in other cities; as a result, the authority has increased the FSI to 5, intended to spur development in these newly developing high-tech sectors.

With significant export potential seen in the region, DCPR has special provisions for the development of Smart FinTech Centers (Regulation 33-13A), IT/ITeS complexes (Regulation 33-13), and Biotechnology units (Regulation 33-17).

No.	Building Type	Permission Clause	Additional FSI norms
1	Biotechnology Unit	Built by any public entity such as MHADA, SEEPZ, MIDC, SICOM, CIDCO or their joint venture with minimum 11% stake	FSI 3, 4, 5 for road frontage 12, 18, 30M respectively * On payment of premium of 50% of land price as per ASR
2	Smart Fin-Tech Centre	85% area for Smart Fin-tech firms No amenities space to be left for plots upto 2 Ha; Minimum road width to be 18m	FSI of 3.0 for Plot upto 200,000 sqm* FSI of 4.0 for plot more than 200,000 sqm* * On payment of 40% premium on land rate as per ASR
3	IT/ITeS Establishment	80% area for IT/ITeS firms 2% area for startup incubation	FSI 3, 4, 5 for road frontage 12, 18, 27M respectively* * On payment of premium of 40% of land price as per ASR

(Source: DCPR 2034 Unleashing MUMBAI'S Economic Potential
(Report by Cushman & Wakefield)

Bengaluru: The FSI ranges from 2.5 to 4 in Bengaluru for commercial properties, depending on the zone.

The Karnataka government approved premium FSI in 2020. The table below shows Premium FSI regulations.

Width of Road Adjacent to Plot/Building	Premium FSI in Bengaluru
30-40 ft.	20%
40-60 ft.	30%
Over 60 ft.	40%

Pune: Regulations for the city follow the UDCPR. In case of Pune, the state government adopted a transit-oriented development strategy in Pune in March 2019, when the policy states a radius of 500 metres around Pune's metro stations & the **maximum FSI permitted in the city is 4.**

Central Business District (CBD)

Central Business District (CBD) is a universally used term in commercial real estate. It is defined as a city's functional area with the maximum concentration of commercial, retail and business centres. Geographically, it coincides with the city centre and is the focal point for the city's transportation networks. It has a maximum urban density than other town districts and offers a healthy environment for various commercial activities.

CBDs offer the best infrastructure for a conducive business environment, such as quality workspaces, multi-storey buildings, quality workspaces, efficient connectivity, adequate electricity and water supply, and parking facilities. Therefore, the average per square feet rate in CBDs is higher than in other commercial centres in the city.

One of India's largest, most modern and most famous CBD is The Bandra Kurla Complex in Mumbai. And in the same city, there is Nariman Point, other CBDs include Andheri and Parel. CBDs are often called "City Centers" or elsewhere "Downtown" in India. In New Delhi, the CBD is Connaught Place. The main CBDs of Chennai are Parry's Corner and Nungambakkam. Bangalore has four famous business districts: UB City, Brigade Gateway, Koramangala, Indiranagar and

Electronic City. Lucknow has mainly three business districts: the famous Hazratganj Market, Gomti Nagar Extension (the extended area of Gomti Nagar) and Aminabad in old Lucknow.

Case Studies of Central Business Districts

1. Bandra Kurla Complex (BKC)

Bandra Kurla Complex (BKC) is centrally located between the two locations, Kurla in the east and Bandra in the west: hence the name "Bandra Kurla Complex". The complex was developed and regulated by MMRDA (Mumbai Metropolitan Region Development Authority) as the special planning authority in 1977; to create an alternative to the Central Business District, which was initially located at Nariman Point. BKC, has now become the main Central Business District in Mumbai, and here's why:

a. Lack of space in Nariman Point for companies looking at large expanses of land, like 30,000 to 40,000 square feet, and amenities like sufficient parking space, gymnasiums, and food courts.

b. BKC lies closer geographically to the heart of the city, compared to Nariman Point, located at the southernmost tip of the city. Domestic and international airports are located much closer to the Bandra Kurla Complex.

c. Most buildings in Nariman Point are more than 30 years old, whereas of the 29 buildings in Mumbai that have received Leadership in Energy and Environmental Design ratings, an urban design standard, BKC has seven of them, with either gold or platinum ratings. These buildings score highly in energy efficiency, water efficiency and have better indoor environmental quality.

BKC houses several commercial buildings, including the National Stock Exchange, SEBI, Punjab National Bank, Twitter India, Amazon.com, Spotify, ICICI Bank, State Bank of India, Kotak Mahindra Bank, Dhirubhai Ambani International School, Institute of Chartered Accountants of India, Fortune 2000, Jio World Drive, Jio World Centre and Jio World Garden. It also hosts the first Apple Store in India called 'Apple BKC'. More than 400,000 (4 lakhs) people work in various offices throughout the BKC.

2. Connaught Place, New Delhi

Connaught Place, known as Rajiv Chowk, is one of India's main commercial, finance and business districts. This area in New Delhi is home to the headquarters of many well-known Indian companies. It is a popular destination for shopping, nightlife, and tourism. It is originally designed to showcase Lutyens' Delhi and features a prominent Central Business District. The New Delhi Municipal Council (NDMC) has jurisdiction under this area and is highly prioritised in terms of funds for maintenance and upkeep.

3. Bengaluru CBD

The central business district of Bengaluru is a 6 km radius area around Vidhan Soudha, the State legislature of Karnataka. It's the core commercial area of Bangalore, founded by Kempegowda of the Vijayanagara Empire. Most of this land is used by the Indian Army and commercial establishments, with plans to construct skyscrapers. It has several high-rises, including World Trade Center Bangalore and UB Tower. Additionally, it features cultural heritage sites such as the Bangalore Fort and the Bangalore Pete.

Among the many attractive features of the CBD are parks, government offices, educational institutions, business houses, hotels, shopping destinations, stadiums, museums, temples, churches and mosques, entertainment zones and art galleries. Brigade Road and MG Road, located in the CBD, are among India's most expensive shopping areas. The Collection in UB City is one of the first luxury shopping malls in South India.

Manyata Embassy Business Park, or Manyata Tech Park, is a software technology park in Nagawara (near Hebbal) on Outer Ring Road, Bengaluru, Karnataka, India. The park covers an area of 300 acres (1.2 km^2) and has a building area of 9.8 million square feet. As of November 2017, it has a workforce of over 150,000 professionals. Some of the tenant companies include Cognizant, Victoria's Secret, Rolls-Royce, Harman, Justdial.com, Harman Kardon, L&T, Nvidia, Nokia Networks, Alcatel-Lucent, WSP, and AXA.

4. Central Business District (CBD)- Singapore

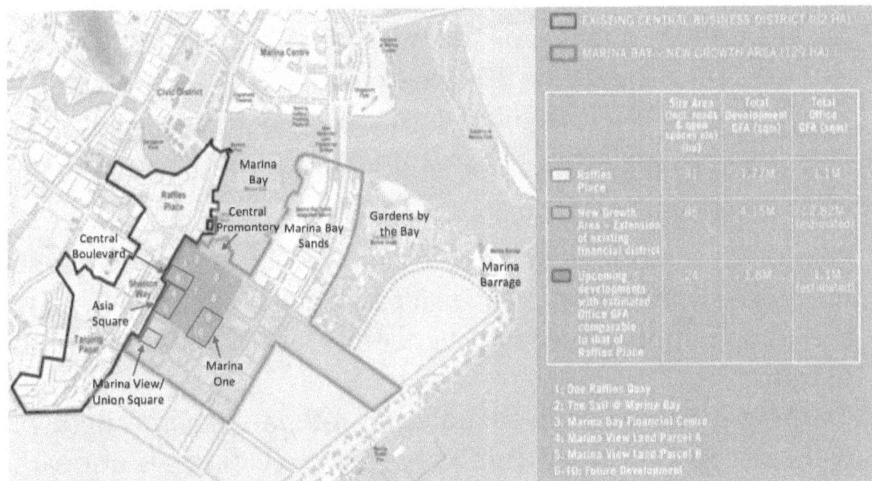

Exhibit 5: Marina Bay New Growth Area
Source: Adapted from URA. "Office Space in Singapore Set to Double." Skyline, March-April, 2008.

Downtown Core is the Central Area's urban core, which contains the CBD and its surrounding developments. Jurong Lake District is known as Singapore's second CBD, spanning from Raffles Place along Shenton Way/Robinson Road/Cecil Street to the Tanjong Pagar and Anson subzones.

The 360-hectare Marina Bay region, next to Singapore's current Central Economic District (CBD), was created to expand the CBD and promote Singapore's development as a major international financial and business centre. According to the Urban Redevelopment Authority (URA), the goal for Marina Bay was to create a vibrant community where people could live, work, and play all the time. The district was anticipated to draw new investments, tourists, and talent and act as a public leisure area for Singaporeans.

The motivation approaches, policy and methods of execution that went into the creation of Marina Bay are covered in this case study. The case study, in particular, concentrates on the 85-ha Marina Bay region designated as the new commercial and financial centre.

CBD Incentive Scheme

The SDI (Strategic Development Incentive) Scheme and the CBD Incentive Scheme both seek to promote Singapore's strategic districts' revitalisation. Sites that are located in the specified areas for the CBD Incentive Scheme will follow its rules and will not be taken into consideration under the SDI Scheme.

The CBD Incentive Scheme aims to encourage the conversion of pre-existing and older office developments into mixed-use developments to help rejuvenate the CBD by:

- Providing a mixed diversity of uses, such as including more residences, hotels, and creative lifestyle possibilities;
- Providing better connectivity to nearby developments and nodes of transport;
- Creating a more people-friendly and intimate environment with wide streets and open public spaces, providing an appeal for people to work and live in.

Strategic Development Incentive (SDI)

If it satisfies the requirements, building owners of projects in key parts of Singapore may employ the SDI Scheme in their applications for redevelopment. According to the SDI Scheme, deviations from the following planning criteria may be taken into account:

- Gross Floor Area
- Quantum of Land Use
- Building Elevation

Building owners may submit applications to the SDI Scheme for projects in Singapore's important locales that satisfy the requirements.

In keeping with the overall planning objective to revitalise these districts, proposals to redevelop existing projects in the Orchard Road, Marina Centre and the Central Business District (CBD) are welcomed. Sites included in the CBD Incentive Scheme's designated areas will follow its guidelines rather than the SDI scheme.

5. Midtown Manhattan

Midtown Manhattan is the main central business district of New York City's borough of Manhattan. It boasts some of the city's most iconic buildings, namely the Empire State Building, the headquarters of the United Nations, the Chrysler Building, the Grand Central Terminal, and the Rockefeller Centre. It is also home to popular tourist destinations like Broadway, Times Square, and Koreatown. In Midtown Manhattan, Penn Station is the busiest transportation hub in the Western Hemisphere.

Midtown Manhattan has one of the largest Central Business Districts in the world and is among the most expensive real estate locations on the planet. 'Fifth Avenue' in Midtown Manhattan has the highest rents (retail) in the world, with an average of US$3,000 per square foot ($32,000/m2) in 2017. However, due to increased retail space prices, there are also many vacant storefronts in the area. Midtown is the largest commercial, entertainment, and media centre in the United States and is also growing as a financial and fintech centre.

The tallest hotels and apartment towers are located in Midtown. This area is home to commuters, residents working in offices, hotels, retail establishments, tourists, and students. Located in the heart of the Broadway Theatre District, Times Square is a bustling hub of the global entertainment industry, brightly illuminated and full of life.

Chapter 4

FSI: Malls & Social Infrastructure

Introduction

In recent years, the Indian retail landscape has witnessed a significant transformation with the rise of malls as prominent shopping destinations. These sprawling complexes, offering a blend of retail, entertainment, and recreational facilities, have become integral parts of urban centres across the country. Behind the success and evolution of these malls lies a complex interplay between Development Control Rules (DCR) and Floor Space Index (FSI) regulations, which govern the planning and construction of these commercial spaces.

Development Control Rules (DCR) play a significant role in shaping the success of a mall. Here are some ways in which DCR can influence the success of a mall:

Zoning and Land Use: DCR determines the zoning regulations and land use categories for different areas. DCR ensures that appropriate locations are available for their establishment by designating specific zones for commercial developments, including malls. This helps attract the right mix of tenants, create a conducive environment for retail and entertainment activities, and ensure the mall's viability.

Floor Space Index (FSI) and Built-up Area: DCR sets guidelines for FSI, which determines the permissible built-up area on a given plot of land. Higher FSI allowances can allow developers to create spacious and well-designed malls. Adequate floor space is essential for accommodating various retail stores, entertainment facilities, dining options, and common areas, contributing to a better shopping experience and the overall success of the mall.

Parking and Access: DCR typically includes provisions for parking requirements and access to the mall. Sufficient parking spaces and well-planned access points are crucial for attracting customers and ensuring convenience. Adequate parking facilities, including surface and multi-level parking, as mandated by DCR, can enhance the mall's appeal and encourage more visitors.

Setbacks and Open Spaces: DCR often includes regulations related to setbacks and open spaces around the mall. These provisions help create a visually pleasing environment, allowing for landscaping, pedestrian-friendly pathways, and outdoor seating areas. Well-designed open spaces can enhance the ambience of the mall, providing opportunities for leisure activities and social interactions.

Amenities and Infrastructure: DCR may prescribe requirements for essential amenities and infrastructure, such as water supply, sewage systems, electricity, and waste management. Adequate provision of these services is crucial for the smooth functioning of the mall and ensuring a pleasant experience for visitors.

Design and Aesthetics: Some DCR guidelines may focus on architectural design, façade treatment, signage regulations, and other aesthetic considerations. These guidelines help maintain a visually appealing and harmonious streetscape, enhancing the overall appeal and attractiveness of the mall.

Evolution of malls in India

The Indian Mall story began in the early 2000s with just three malls in the country. Over 650 malls offer clean, vibrant, climate-controlled, and technology-enabled spaces with many brands today. Despite facing challenges from e-commerce, economic slowdowns, and policy changes, mall developers remained focused and worked hard to retain footfalls. They introduced new brands and experiences to attract and retain visitors, improving malls across Tier I, II, and III cities.

The mall culture has become deeply entrenched in India, offering dedicated spaces for shopping, entertainment, dining, and cinema. The growth of malls is driven by factors such as rapid urbanisation, increasing disposable incomes, and lifestyle changes in middle-class society. Major cities like Gurgaon, Noida, Greater Noida, Delhi, Mumbai, Chennai, Bengaluru, and Pune have seen the maximum number of malls. However, retail expansion is also taking place in Tier II cities like Lucknow, Coimbatore, Chandigarh, Mangalore, and Ahmedabad, attracting domestic and overseas retailers.

Top-performing Malls in India and International Locations

Mall Name	Location	Country	Unique Selling Point (USP)	Design Philosophy
Select Citywalk	New Delhi	India	Premium brands, high-end shopping experience	Contemporary architecture with open-air spaces
DLF Mall of India	Noida	India	Largest mall in India, diverse retail offerings	Modern and spacious design with themed zones
High Street Phoenix	Mumbai	India	Integrated entertainment, dining, and shopping	Urban-style design with trendy aesthetics
UB City	Bangalore	India	Luxury brands, upscale dining and nightlife	Modern and luxurious ambience
Mall of Emirates	Dubai	UAE	Indoor ski slope, extensive retail and dining	Grand and opulent design with Arabic influences
Mall of America	Minnesota	USA	The largest mall in the USA, a wide range of retailers	Sprawling layout with themed areas and attractions

Mall Name	Location	Country	Unique Selling Point (USP)	Design Philosophy
West Edmonton Mall	Edmonton	Canada	Indoor amusement park, water park, and shopping	A unique blend of retail, entertainment, and leisure
ION Orchard	Singapore	Singapore	High-end fashion, luxury brands, rooftop garden	Sleek and contemporary design with green spaces
Mall of Asia	Pasay City	Philippines	Oceanarium, IMAX theatre, vast retail selection	Modern architecture with waterfront views
Lotte World Mall	Seoul	South Korea	Indoor theme park, duty-free shopping	Futuristic design with emphasis on entertainment

Based on the above table, it can be observed that the common elements among these malls include:

Focus on Entertainment: Many malls prioritise entertainment and recreational facilities alongside retail spaces. They incorporate theme parks, indoor ski slopes, waterfront promenades, and large-scale events to enhance the overall experience for visitors.

Innovative Design: These malls often showcase creative and unique architectural elements that set them apart. They aim to create visually striking spaces that captivate visitors and provide a memorable environment.

Emphasis on Luxury and High-end Brands: Several malls strongly focus on luxury retail and high-end brands catering to affluent consumers. They aim to create an upscale ambience and offer a premium shopping experience.

DCR and FSI policies can play a role in incorporating these elements in mall design and development. By providing higher FSI allowances for commercial and entertainment spaces within malls, developers can include larger entertainment zones, innovative architectural features, and spacious retail areas.

Higher FSI can also include additional amenities and recreational facilities, such as cinemas, food courts, gaming zones, and event spaces. This enables malls to offer diverse experiences beyond traditional retail, enhancing their attractiveness to visitors.

Additionally, FSI policies can incentivise developers to focus on creating aesthetically pleasing and architecturally innovative designs by allowing for taller structures or unique architectural features. This can contribute to the creation of iconic and visually striking mall designs.

Overall, FSI policies that encourage and accommodate the incorporation of entertainment, innovative design, and luxury retail can help create vibrant and successful malls that cater to consumers' evolving needs and preferences.

(fig: Dubai Mall)

Nexus REIT Ushers in a New Era for Indian Malls

Nexus Select Trust REIT has achieved a significant milestone as it becomes the first REIT in India supported by retail real estate assets that generate rent. This opens up a new chapter for the Indian mall industry, providing investors the chance to invest in its expansion. India's total Grade A mall stock is around 93 MSF. Out of this, more than 50% are in NCR and MMR. Nexus has 17 Malls in its portfolio and has 9.8 MSF of stock.

Retail-REIT could help shape development policy for malls in India by demonstrating the potential for growth and investment in the retail real estate industry. As the first REIT backed by rent-yielding retail real estate assets in India, Nexus REIT is a model for other companies looking to enter the market.

The success of Nexus REIT's IPO and its strong performance in the market could encourage policymakers to create a more favourable regulatory environment for the development of malls and other retail real estate assets. This could include streamlining the approval process for new products, providing tax incentives for investment in the industry, and promoting public-private partnerships to support the growth of the retail real estate sector.

Importance of Social Infrastructure

Enhancing Quality of Life: Social infrastructure facilities such as schools, hospitals, parks, community centres, libraries, and cultural institutions contribute to improving the quality of life for residents. Access to education, healthcare, recreational spaces, and cultural activities enhances social well-being, promotes personal growth, and fosters community belonging.

Promoting Social Cohesion: Social infrastructure provides spaces and opportunities for people to come together, interact, and engage with one another. It creates a sense of community and fosters social cohesion, enabling residents to build relationships, share experiences, and collaborate on common interests or goals. This sense of belonging and social interaction is crucial for creating resilient and inclusive communities.

Supporting Economic Development: Social infrastructure facilities play an integral role in driving economic growth and development. Access to quality education and vocational training centres equips people to develop the skills and necessary knowledge to participate in the workforce and contribute to the economy. Healthcare facilities ensure a healthy and productive workforce, while cultural and recreational amenities contribute to the tourism industry and local businesses.

Ensuring Equity and Social Justice: Social infrastructure helps address societal inequalities and promotes social justice. It ensures that essential services and opportunities are accessible to all residents, regardless of socio-economic background or geographic location. Schools, libraries, and community centres act as equalisers by providing opportunities for learning, skill development, and social inclusion.

Improving Public Health and Well-being: Social infrastructure, particularly healthcare facilities, is critical in improving public health outcomes. Accessible and well-equipped hospitals, clinics, and healthcare centres ensure timely and quality healthcare services for residents. Additionally, the availability of parks, recreational spaces, and sports complexes promotes physical activity, mental well-being, and a healthier lifestyle.

Attracting Investments and Talent: Well-developed social infrastructure is crucial in attracting investments and skilled talent to a region. Investors and businesses are more likely to establish themselves in areas with a robust social infrastructure network that can cater to the needs of their employees and their families. Similarly, talented individuals are drawn to cities and communities that offer quality education, healthcare, and recreational opportunities.

Resilience and Disaster Preparedness: Social infrastructure plays a vital role in building resilient communities capable of withstanding and recovering from disasters. Adequate healthcare facilities, emergency response systems, and evacuation centres are essential for managing and mitigating the impact of natural or artificial disasters. Social infrastructure planning should incorporate disaster resilience measures to ensure the safety and well-being of the community during challenging times.

Chapter 5

FSI: Industries, Data Centre, IT and ITES

Important Terms

1. **Warehouse:** A warehouse is a large building or facility used to store, organise, and distribute goods and materials. It serves as a central location where products and inventory are stored before they are shipped to customers, retailers, or other distribution centres.

2. **Cold-Storage:** Cold storage is a method of keeping or storing products, typically perishable goods or sensitive materials, at low temperatures to maintain their quality, integrity, or viability over an extended time. It entails using chilling or freezing techniques to create a controlled environment that

inhibits microbe development, pauses chemical processes, and lowers the pace of spoiling or degradation.

3. **Industrial Logistic Park:** An industrial logistics park is a specialised area or facility designed to support industrial businesses' logistics and transportation needs. It provides a comprehensive infrastructure and services for storing, distributing, and moving goods.

   These parks are located near major transportation routes, such as highways, railways, and ports, to facilitate efficient transportation and connectivity with suppliers and customers.

   Industrial logistics parks often offer a range of amenities and services, including warehousing facilities, distribution centres, loading docks, customs clearance, and value-added services like packaging and labelling.

   Industrial logistics parks enhance operational efficiency, reduce transportation costs, and improve supply chain responsiveness, making them attractive for businesses seeking streamlined logistics operations and strategic advantages.

(Srijan Industrial Logistics Park, Kolkata)

4. **Data Centre:** A data centre is a physical space that contains IT infrastructure for creating, operating, and providing applications and services. It also stores and manages the data required for these applications and services. Over time, data centres have transformed from privately-owned, on-site facilities for single companies to remote facilities owned by cloud service providers. These providers house virtualized IT infrastructure that multiple companies and customers share.

About the IT Industry

The Information Technology Industry is a major contributor to India's economy, making up 9.3% of the country's GDP. It is one of the largest sectors in India and plays a critical role in the country's economic growth. Additionally, India's IT industry leads the global outsourcing market, accounting for an impressive 56%.

The Maharashtra Advantage

Maharashtra has become a major centre for technology and innovation since the 1990s. The state has established itself as a major hub for IT & ITeS, electronics, and captive business outsourcing industries, giving it a competitive edge in both domestic and global markets.

Maharashtra's IT &ITES policy-2023

Year	Focus Areas	Key Strategic Drivers
2023	• IT Software Products • Data Centers • IT Enabled Services • AVGC & Emerging Technologies • IT & ITeS Supporting services • Integrated IT Townships • Infrastructure for Walk to Work concept	• Unified single Window System for all IT & ITeS Segments • Dispersal of IT & ITeS segments to all parts of the State • Turbo charging Emerging tech, AVGC, Green IT, Innovation& Start up, Data Centre etc. • Technology Ambassador to promote Brand Maharashtra through improved governance • Renewed focus on IT exports through start-ups & MSMEs

Promotion of IT & ITeS Infrastructure – IT Townships and IT Parks

- **Development Incentives:**

To promote the growth and development of IT & ITeS infrastructure in the state, dedicated incentives have been delineated specific to IT Townships and IT Parks.

- **Additional FSI and Space Utilisation of IT Parks:**

Sr. No	Road Width (m)	Maximum Permissible FSI Greater Mumbai Region	Maximum Permissible FSI Rest of Maharashtra
1	12	Up to 3	Up to 3
2	18	Up to 4	Up to 3.5
3	27	Up to 5	Up to 4

Additional FSI Limit shall be applicable as above or as per the Local DCR norms, whichever is higher, excluding in Agriculture Zone, NDZ, or any others special zone, declared by Urban Development Department, where the maximum Additional Floor Space Index limit shall remain applicable as per prevailing Development Control Regulation.

Relevant DCRs, DCPRs & UDCPRs will be amended accordingly by all concerned Special Planning Authorities (SPAs).

Premium for additional Floor Space index for IT Park

a) For Brihanmumbai Municipal Corporation Area:

As per Development Control and Promotion Regulations-2034, all Public and Private Information Technology Parks in the Brihanmumbai Municipal Corporation area; Additional FSI shall be admissible by levying a premium at the rate of 50 % of prevailing rate of premium to be charged for the area as mentioned in the respective DCPRs.

b) For the Rest of Maharashtra:

i.   Areas in Vidharbha, Marathwada, Dhule, Nandurbar, Ratnagiri and Sindhudurg, no premium will be charged for additional Floor Space Index (FSI).

ii. As per Unified Development Control & Promotion Rules (UDCPR) & Special Planning Authority DCRs, the additional FSI shall be permissible to all Public & Private IT Parks / AVGC Parks by levying a premium at the rate of 50 % of prevailing rate of premium for areas other than (a) and (b)(I)

c) For Central Business District:

If any special planning authority declared any area as a Central Business District as per applicable DCR norms; all registered public and private Information Technology parks in the particular CBDs will be entitled for permissible additional FSI by levying a premium at the rate of 50 % of the existing rate of premium as mentioned in the DCPR of Central Business District.

Other applicable FSI's like Fungible, Ancillary FSI will be applicable as per the local applicable DCR/UDCPR/DCPR norms. The developer will be allowed to pay the premium, development charges, ancillary charges and other charges for the increased additional FSI for the IT Park in instalments.

- **Establishment of Integrated Information Technology Townships (IITTs)**

Minimum Land requirement: Ten acres contiguous land with staggered proportion of usage component. 50% for IT & ITeS use and 50% for usage without any restriction as per prevailing norms.

MIDC will be declared as Special Planning Authority throughout the State excluding CIDCO areas.

If the area of Integrated Information Technology Township is up from 10 acres to 25 acres, the period of completion of the project will be 7.5 years and if the area is more than 25 acres, this period will be 10 years. In case of delay the extension will be considered subject to approval of the Committee constituted in this regard.

Staggered payment facility for premium to be paid for additional FSI. This is allowed in two instalments with the stipulation that the entire premium is paid within a year or the date of obtaining the Occupancy / Part Occupancy certificate whichever is earlier.

Integrated IT Townships are permitted in any zone across the state. The option will be given to the developer for project implementation with or without zone conversion of the said area. However, the FSI norms will continue to remain as per prevailing classification of the area as per DCR in force viz. for projects proposed to be set up in No development zone, Green Zone, Special zone etc.

- **Critical Infrastructure Fund:** The State Government shall create a separate fund viz. "Critical Infrastructure Fund for IT & ITeS Industries" from the premium paid for availing additional FSI by the Developers of the Private IT Parks. This fund shall be utilised only for creation of Critical Infrastructure for IT & ITeS Industries.
- **Power Tariff:** Power consumed will be charged at industrial rate for the common facilities in the IT Park (such as lobbies, central air conditioning, lifts, escalators, effluent treatment plant, washrooms, cafeterias, gymnasium, training rooms etc.) which are used by the units, excluding support service areas after the registration is granted to the IT park by the Directorate of Industries and Development Commissioner of the SEZ for an IT SEZ.
- **Green IT Awards:** Awards shall be conferred to IT & ITeS Parks and Units across different categories for demonstrated efficient natural resource management every year on 20th August on the State Information Technology Day.

Promotion of Data Centres

Mumbai has the highest number of undersea data-cable landing stations in India, making it a key link for the Asia Pacific Region. With 42% of the total DC capacity in the country, Mumbai is a major driver for market expansion. The Government of Maharashtra aims to develop Zone I cities, particularly Mumbai and Navi Mumbai, into Data Center Hubs given their reliable power supply, numerous undersea cable landings, and highly skilled workforce. Zone I is poised to become Asia-Pacific's data centre hub.

Incentives to support Data Centres:

- **Stamp Duty Exemption**

  When purchasing land or premises to set up or expand a new data centre, there is a 100% stamp duty exemption. This exemption also applies to actions such as hypothecation, pawn, pledge, deposit of title deeds, conveyance, lease, assignment of lease, leave and licence agreement, merger, de-merger, and reconstruction.

- **Electricity duty exemption**

  Permanently for New and Existing Data Center Units registered with the Directorate of Industries established in the state, shall be exempted permanently from payment of electricity duty.

- **Power Tariff Subsidy**

  a. All Data Centres registered with the Directorate of Industries will be supplied power at Industrial Tariff from the date of starting of the operations.

  b. Subsidy at INR 1 per unit for 5 years for new Data Centre Units located in areas other than Zone- I.

- **Setting up of data centre in any Zone**

  Data centres will be allowed to set up in any zone (including residential, No development zone and green zone etc.)

- **Essential Services Status**

  Data centres will be classified as essential services under the Essential Services and Maintenance Act (ESMA) due to their critical operations that cannot be disrupted.

- **Parking norms**

  Exemption from standard parking norms that are necessary for other IT parks/ IT units. The norm for parking space inside the park will be modified as one vehicle per 400 sq. m. of built-up space.

- **Power Distribution Licences**

  MIDC to seek Distribution Licence for MIDC Areas in pursuance of recommendation of the Government of Maharashtra under Section 13 of Electricity Act, 2003 to undertake Distribution Business in its notified areas.

- **Renewable Energy Use**

  Permitted to avail renewable energy under open access system after paying cost component to DISCOMs as per existing government norms.

- **Captive Power Farms**

  Companies willing to establish captive power farms (wind/solar) will be facilitated by the government in line with the prevailing policy of the Energy Department in this regard.

- **Power Supply**

  Data Centres shall be exempted from state's statutory power cuts & will be given continuous power supply 24X7X365.

- **Open Access**

  a. As electricity is a major contributor of operational expenses of a Data Centre, the state shall allow Data Center parks to get power through open access.

  b. In MIDC areas, MIDC will be the power distribution agency to all Data Centres.

- **Dial before dig**

  Dial-before-Dig Policy is designed to assist Data Centres in minimising downtime. This service safeguards the network of underground lines and cables, guaranteeing the safety of individuals working around this infrastructure.

- **Infrastructure Status**

  Data Centres shall be given infrastructure status on a par with sectors such as railways, roadways, and power, to enable the industry to avail benefits such as long-term credit from lenders at easier terms.

- **Continuous Water Supply**

  For Data Centres in the area of any Industrial Area Development Authority such as MIDC, it will ensure 24X7 uninterrupted water supply to the data centre units both inside and outside the DC Park. To the extent possible, data centre units will recycle the water to minimise their water requirements.

- **FSI Norms**

  Data Centres, being a unique activity will be permitted to avail additional FSI.

F.S.I. Policies Related to Industries, Warehouses and Data Centres

1. National Data Centre Policy 2021
2. Maharashtra Industrial Policy 2019
3. Karnataka Industrial Policy 2020-25
4. Telangana Industrial Strategy 2020-25
5. The Delhi Master Plan 2021
6. Gujarat Industrial Policy 2020
7. Rajasthan Industrial Policy 2019

Policies related to Data Centres in India vs Cities across the Globe

- **India:**

1. National Data Centre Policy 2021

2. Make in India policy

3. Digital India initiative

4. Maharashtra Industrial Policy 2019

5. Karnataka Industrial Policy 2020-25

- **Singapore:**

1. Green Data Centre Standard

2. Carbon Pricing Act

3. Economic Development Board's Data Centre Park initiative

4. Data Centre Park Development Guidebook

5. Sustainable Data Centre Technical Guide

- **USA:**

1. Tax incentives for data centre development in several states, such as Virginia, Texas, and Oregon

2. Energy Star rating for data centres

3. Better Buildings Challenge for data centres

4. North Carolina Data Centre Energy Efficiency Program

- **UK:**

1. UK Data Centre Code of Conduct

2. Digital Infrastructure Investment Fund

3. Industrial Strategy White Paper

4. Climate Change Act

5. Building Regulations Part L

- **China:**

1. Made in China 2025 initiative

2. National Data Center Development Plan

3. Green Data Centre Policy

4. Energy Efficiency Label for Data Centres

5. Energy Efficiency Regulations for Industrial Enterprises

Ideal Warehousing Regulations - Unified Development Control and Planning Regulations (UDCPR)

1. For optimal warehouse design, it is recommended to maintain a land-to-building ratio between 1.7:1 to 2:1 in lineal metres.
2. A building aspect ratio of 1.7:1 to 2:1. The ideal warehouse height at the springing line is between 9.5-10.5 metres.
3. The recommended pallet per square metre ratio is 1 to 1.2 with conventional storage racking.
4. Ensure that there is ample truck turning space of 30-40 metres.
5. It is also advisable to allocate 20 to 25% of the warehouse floor for non-storage operations such as receiving, dispatching, and staging.

Chapter 6

Special Economic Zones

Few important terms

- **Special Economic Zone:** SEZ (Special Economic Zone) is a geographical area in a country under special economic regulations and policies designed to facilitate trade, attract foreign investment, and stimulate economic growth. Governments often establish SEZs as part of their financial plans.

- **Export-Oriented Units:** Export Oriented Units, also known as EOUs, are special factories or companies set up in some countries to help businesses sell their products to other countries. These units make it easier for companies to export their goods and boost their sales internationally.

  EOUs receive special advantages and benefits from the government to make their products more competitive and attractive in the global market. These benefits include tax breaks, reduced customs duties, simplified export procedures, and lower-cost access to infrastructure and utilities. By providing these incentives, governments hope to attract more foreign buyers and increase the country's exports, leading to economic growth, employment growth, and increased foreign exchange earnings.

- **Integrated Industrial Area:** An integrated industrial area is where different factories, industries, and related facilities are located together. It is designed to promote efficiency and collaboration among the businesses operating within it. In these areas, companies from different sectors and industries are grouped based on certain criteria, such as the type of products they produce or the services they provide. This clustering allows for easier access to resources, shared infrastructure, and common services that can benefit all the businesses in the area.

Global Perspective on SEZs

1. Singapore: Singapore has designed one-north Singapore, the first innovation district in the ASEAN. The first Asian industrial park was founded in Singapore in 1951.

A government agency known as The Singapore Economic Development Board (EDB) aims to strengthen Singapore's position as a leading hub for business, innovation, and talent on a global scale. It operates under the Ministry of Trade and Industry.

Total number of Economic Zones in Singapore - 6

Number of Industrial Parks - 2

Number of Special Economic Zones - 0

Number of Eco-Industrial Parks - 1

Number of Technology Parks - 2

Number of Innovation Districts - 1

(Free Trade Zones) Singapore established FTZs in 1969 to support its goal of becoming a hub for entrepot trading and transhipment activities. Over time, the objectives of these zones have broadened. FTZs in Singapore are specific areas where no duties or taxes are charged on goods when they are received, kept, or sold within the zone.

Advantages of FTZ:-

* Import Permit is not needed in FTZs
* No Customs Duties are levied on Goods Imported into FTZs
* No Goods and Services Tax on Imports
* Duty and import GST only apply if you use goods in Singapore's FTZ or sell/use them locally outside of it.
* Designated areas are to be used for storage of goods without the need for customs documentation until their sale. Furthermore, minimal customs procedures are necessary for their treatment and re-exportation.

Nine Singapore free trade zones exist, as of 2023:

1. Airport Logistics Park of Singapore
2. Brani Terminal
3. Changi Airport Cargo Terminal Complex
4. Jurong Port (including Pulau Damar Laut)
5. Keppel Distripark
6. Keppel Distripark Linkbridge
7. Pasir Panjang Terminal
8. Sembawang Wharves
9. Tanjong Pagar Terminal and Keppel Terminal

2. China: In the 1980s, China implemented its "reform and opening up" policy, which led to the creation of SEZs in four coastal cities (Shenzhen, Zhuhai, Shantou, and Xiamen) near Hong Kong, Macao, and Taiwan. As foreign investment in these cities increased, more zones were established in other coastal cities. Later, in the 1990s and 2000s, two additional waves of SEZ expansion occurred, which focused on promoting regional development in inland and western areas of China.

Special Policy Framework: The SEZs enjoyed a different policy framework from the rest of the country. This framework provided greater freedom in enacting reforms and experimenting with new policies. SEZs had greater decision-making autonomy, which aided economic development and attracted foreign enterprises.

Objectives, Benchmarks, and Competition - SEZs in China were normally set up in batches—initially four—and then the number increased rapidly. Despite many of these zones, they have clear goals and targets for GDP growth, exports, employment, revenues, and FDI generation. These expectations put a great deal of pressure and responsibility on the shoulders of the government. Meanwhile, the hundreds of SEZs are highly competitive among themselves. Every Special Economic Zone aims to stand out by providing exceptional service, top-notch infrastructure, and an appealing appearance to lure in new businesses and achieve their development objectives. Such competition helps make them more efficient and competitive.

Source: "China's special economic zones: an analysis of policy to reduce regional disparities."

Type of zone by time period	1980s	1990s	2000s	2010s
1. Special Economic Zones (SEZs)	• Shenzhen • Zhuhai • Shantou • Xiamen • Hainan (province)	Industrial upgrading began	Uneven success in upgrading	Uneven success in upgrading • Kashgar • Horgos
2. Economic & Technological Development Zones (ETDZs)	14 coastal cities including: • Shanghai • Ningbo • Nantong • Others	Began industrial upgrading	Transition and diversification to high-tech manufacturing and service	Fully institutionalized and stable
3. High- and New-Technology Zones (HNTZs); Border SEZs		Special zones spread to coastal, central and western border regions • Ruili • Mohan (Yunnan)	Growing and spreading nationally	Uneven success
4. New Free Trade Zones (FTZs) and Overseas Economic and Commercial Cooperation Zones (OECCZs)		Growing gap between coastal and inland/border regions	"Go West" and "Go Global" policies began • China-built SEZs in Africa	Belt & Road Initiative (BRI) launched • Shanghai FTZ • Forest City, Johor, Malaysia • China–Laos (Mohan-Boten) Economic Cooperation Zone (ECZ)

3. USA: Opportunity Zones are economically disadvantaged locations in the United States where tax breaks are offered to promote long-term investments. The Opportunity Zones programme stimulates capital investment, job development, and economic growth in underrepresented neighbourhoods. Opportunity Zones have the following characteristics:

- Tax Advantages: Investors who place capital gains in Qualified Opportunity Funds (QOFs) may be eligible for tax benefits such as deferral and potential reduction of capital gains taxes, as well as potential tax-free growth on investments.
- Community growth: The program encourages economic growth and job creation in low-income neighbourhoods by facilitating private investment.
- Long-Term Investment Focus: Investments in Opportunity Zones often require a long-term commitment to maximising tax benefits, consistent with supporting sustained economic development.

The SEZs in the United States are known as foreign-trade zones. These foreign-trade zones are customs-free. The objective of these zones is to encourage firms to undertake distribution or manufacturing operations at United States facilities rather than elsewhere. Subzones can be established by FTZs for use by individual companies in the area. There are over 500 approved subzones that may undertake manufacturing activities. Several major industries utilise zone procedures, such as oil refining, automotive, electronics, pharmaceuticals, machinery, and equipment.

4. UK: In the United Kingdom, Special Economic Zones (SEZs) are not typically referred to by a specific term or name like in some other countries. They are known as:-

1. Enterprise zones
2. Science Parks and Innovation Districts
3. Free Zones

Enterprise Zones play a major role in attracting foreign investment to England and creating job opportunities nationwide. These zones focus on promoting sustainable growth through advanced technology and entrepreneurship. Businesses in various sectors, including financial services, bio-sciences, digital and creative industries, advanced engineering, automotive, and renewable energy, are located in these zones, strategically placed around centres of excellence.

Case Studies in India

1. Jawaharlal Nehru Port Trust:

Jawaharlal Nehru Port Trust (JNPT) is a crucial player in India's trade and commerce, providing seamless services to international cargo. Its location near Mumbai, Navi Mumbai, and Pune, as well as airports, hotels, and exhibition centres, allows JNPT to address shipper requirements promptly.

JNPT has created a multi-product Special Economic Zone (SEZ) on 277.38 hectares of land owned by JNPT along the Panvel-Uran Road connecting cargo terminals to state highways. This SEZ offers low last-mile costs for export-oriented manufacturers, as it is only 5 km from the port.

The SEZ in the Port has given out 21 plots for co-developers to build 20 MSME units and one FTWZ. Construction has already begun for five of these plots. Two companies, M/s OWS LLP Oil Field Warehouse Pvt. Ltd. and M/s Krish Food Industry (India), have finished their first phase of operations and were approved as operational units by the Development Commissioner of SEEPZ SEZ on June 24, 2020.

2. Mundra Port:

Mundra is India's largest private port and is a significant hub for containers and bulk cargo. The port has been operated by Adani Ports and SEZ Limited (APSEZ) since 2001.

Located in the Northern Gulf of Kutch, Gujarat, on the western coast of India, APSEZ Limited, Mundra is the country's largest privately developed port and a multisector SEZ covering an area of 100 sq. km. Its strategic location en route to major maritime routes makes it a convenient gateway for EXIM trade, particularly for Africa, Middle Eastern countries, Europe and America. It also benefits from its proximity to the land-locked hinterland of North and North-West India, allowing it to service the industry and trade that accounts for almost 70% of the country's total international cargo.

APSEZ Ltd, Mundra handles a diverse range of cargo, including bulk cargo such as coal, wheat, fertiliser, minerals, ores, steel, edible oils, chemicals, and petroleum products, as well as container cargo, automobiles, and crude oil.

Due to its location, Mundra provides an ideal place for product evacuation with the shortest logistics connectivity to the North-Western hinterland, making it the perfect location for cargo export to major destinations like Delhi, Rajasthan, Gujarat, MP, Haryana, Punjab, and HP. The port-based multi-product manufacturing zone is also well connected to major global locations by sea, including the Middle East, Europe, the US, Africa, Indian Subcontinent, and Far East/Southeast Asia.

APSEZ's integrated model helps reduce the time to reach the market and provides considerable cost savings while maintaining quality, delivery times, and safety.

3. Kandla port:

Kandla Port, officially known as Deendayal Port Trust, is located in Kandla, Gujarat, India. It is the largest port in the country by volume. The port is a well-connected rail and road network road. It caters to the trade requirements and provides a gateway port for the export and import of traffic of one of the most highly productive granaries and industrial belts of the country stretching across northern Indian states of Jammu & Kashmir, Punjab, Delhi, Himachal Pradesh, Haryana, Rajasthan, Gujarat and parts of Madhya Pradesh, Uttaranchal and Uttar Pradesh. Kandla Port houses a Special Economic Zone known as the Kandla Special Economic Zone (KASEZ).

KASEZ provides a range of incentives and benefits to businesses, including tax concessions, simplified customs procedures, and infrastructure support, promoting industrial growth and attracting investment.

KASEZ is on the path to becoming a green SEZ. In this context, to reduce vehicular pollution, replacing all motorised vehicles like buses and auto rickshaws with battery-operated vehicles/bicycles as far as possible for commuting within the zone is proposed.

4. Reliance MET:

Reliance MET (Model Economic Township) is a large-scale industrial project developed by Reliance Industries Limited in the Jhajjar district in Haryana, India. It is designed as an integrated industrial township spread over around 8,000 acres (32 square kilometres).

Model Economic Township (MET) project is under the Delhi Mumbai Industrial Corridor (DMIC) Project, and the Haryana Government has recommended it as a node of DMIC. The Model Economic Township project is also connected to the Western Dedicated Freight Corridor (DFC). The company is well-positioned due to its strategic location concerning connectivity and trade. It is expected to attract various companies from several industries, such as warehouses, logistics, footwear etc.

Strategic Location with Excellent Connectivity

- Located in NCR along Delhi's eastern border and North of Gurgaon
- Located ~ 1Hrs. Away from IGI Airport Delhi and ~40 minutes from Gurgaon City

- Excellent Connectivity through KMP Expressway, DFC and Private Freight Terminal (PFT)

Thriving Ecosystem

- ~8250 acres Integrated Township.
- Established an Ecosystem of more than 400 companies
- Social Infrastructure in close proximity, i.e., residential, retail, schools, hospitals etc.
- Approved Japan Industrial Township. Availability of ample skilled workforce.

5. Jamnagar:

Reliance Industries' enormous industrial complex in Jamnagar has revolutionised the city's economy. The complex contains the refinery, petrochemical plants, power generation facilities, and associated infrastructure, which creates jobs and drives economic development. It is noted for its export-oriented industries, particularly in textiles, handicrafts, brass and copper products, and chemical manufacturing. These sectors considerably contribute to foreign trade and export revenues. The strategic location of Jamnagar on the Gulf of Kutch provides advantages for business and logistics by providing access to coastal shipping routes and close to major ports. This position makes export-import and industrial operations easier.

Global Case Studies

1. Jurong Island, Singapore:

Jurong Island is located to the southwest of the main island of Singapore. It powers one of Singapore's key economic sectors, its energy and chemical industry. In 2020, it contributed around 3% of Singapore's GDP and one-fifth of its output. Over 27,000 people work here, including Singaporeans who enjoy well-paying jobs and good career progression. The E&C sector also links strongly to other industries, such as trading and logistics. It helps plug Singapore into the world as an export-oriented sector, helping to maintain and increase its relevance and giving the world a stake in the city-state's success. Jurong Island has attracted over S$50 billion in investments so far. As part of the Singapore Green Plan 2030, Jurong Island (JI) will be transformed into a sustainable Energy & Chemicals (E&C) park.

2. Zona Franca de Manaus (Manaus Free Trade Zone), Brazil:

The Manaus Free Trade Zone (Zona Franca de Manaus) is a special economic zone located in Manaus, in Amazonas, Brazil. Established in 1967, it was created to stimulate economic development in the Amazon region and promote industrialisation in a remote area with limited infrastructure.

The Manaus Industrial Complex is home to around 600 advanced industries that provide over 500,000 jobs, primarily in the electronic, two-wheel, and chemical sectors. These industries produce a range of products, including cell phones, audio and video devices, televisions, motorcycles, and concentrates for soft drinks.

Creating the free trade zone in Manaus in the State of Amazonas (Zona Franca de Manaus e Amazônia Occidental) is a success story about promoting economic growth in the Amazon region. Imported foreign goods are tax-free, provided they are consumed within the zone or are exported abroad. These fiscal benefits also apply to certain areas of the Western Amazon region, which cover the states of Acre, Amazonas, Rondônia and Roraima. Mainly due to the Manaus free-trade zone, the area gradually increased its participation in the Brazilian GDP in recent years, now representing the 4th highest GDP in Brazil. It accounts for 1.4% of the country's economy (increased from US$1 bn per year in 1970 to US$35 bn in 2004). Its international airport 'Eduardo Gomes' represents the second largest in Brazil measured by freight tonnes, and its port is the most important cargo handling port in the Amazonas region. The State of Amazonas has experienced significant growth over the last 10 to 20 years, thanks to the free trade zone in Manaus. This growth has exceeded the Brazilian national average.

Chapter 7

Townships

Integrated Township

An integrated township is like a mini-city within a city. It is a planned neighbourhood combining various daily life aspects into one convenient and self-sufficient community. These townships have a mix of residential buildings, commercial spaces, recreational areas, and essential services.

Advantages of Integrated Townships over standalone residential projects

1. Convenience: Everything you need, such as homes, offices, shops, schools, and recreational facilities, is available within proximity, reducing the need for long commutes.
2. Time and cost savings: With various nearby amenities, time and money on transportation expenses is saved by residents.
3. Community living: Integrated townships foster a sense of community and provide opportunities for social interaction and a feeling of belonging.
4. Well-planned infrastructure: These townships are designed with efficient infrastructure, including good road networks, utility systems, and green spaces.
5. Enhanced security: Integrated townships often have security measures, such as gated entries, surveillance systems, and community patrols.
6. Sustainability: These townships emphasise eco-friendly practices, incorporating renewable energy systems, waste management solutions, and water conservation methods.

7. Quality living environment: Integrated townships offer well-maintained surroundings, landscaped parks, and recreational facilities, promoting a healthier and happier lifestyle.
8. Educational and healthcare facilities: Many integrated townships include schools, colleges, and healthcare centres, providing convenience for residents.
9. Reduced traffic congestion: By providing local amenities, integrated townships help reduce traffic congestion in the surrounding areas.
10. Investment potential: Integrated townships often experience appreciation in property value, making them attractive for real estate investment.

Concessions for integrated township projects

The government of Maharashtra encourages the construction of townships by offering concessions to developers who undertake such projects. The Unified Development Control and Promotion Regulations for Maharashtra State (UDCPR) Regulation 14.1.1.13 provides incentives for developers to construct Integrated Township Projects. The concessions offered by the government are listed below:

1. Concession on Stamp Duty: If a project developer buys land for a township project or sells a unit in a constructed township project for the first time, they can get a 50% discount on stamp duty. This discount is only available for the first transaction based on the Maharashtra Stamp Act 1958.
2. Exemption in payment of Development Charges: According to Section 124F (3) of the Maharashtra Regional and Town Planning Act of 1966, Project Developers are partially exempted from paying Development Charges (up to 50%) for developing an Integrated Township Project.
3. Exemption from the ceiling for holding agricultural land: The government of the State is providing an exemption from the agricultural land ceiling prescribed under Section 3 of the Maharashtra Agricultural Lands (Ceiling on Holdings) Act, 1961. This exemption will allow the acquisition of agricultural land to develop an Integrated Township Project.

4. Deemed conversion for Non-Agricultural Land: The Master Layout Plan for the Integrated Township Project designates all included land as non-agricultural, so there is no need for additional permission to use it for non-agricultural purposes under the Maharashtra Land Revenue Code, 1966. Additionally, a 50% exemption from the normal rate for non-agricultural assessment applies to the land being developed for the project.

5. Transfer of agricultural land for townships: In Maharashtra, only agriculturists can buy agricultural land according to Section 63 of the Maharashtra Tenancy and Agricultural Lands Act, 1948 (MTAL). However, Integrated Township Projects are exempted from this rule under Section 63-1A of MTAL. This means that an individual can transfer agricultural land without prior permission from the District Collector if it's for developing an Integrated Township Project. Moreover, the Revenue and Forest Department of the State Government may grant government land to the developer if their already owned lands surround it and comply with the rules and regulations.

6. Other Concessions: The Indian government's Ministry of Commerce & Industry Department of Industrial Policy & Promotion SIA (FC Division) has allowed Foreign Direct Investment of up to 100% in Integrated Township Projects through Press Note No.4 (2001 series). However, certain guidelines must be followed to qualify for this permission.

Case Studies of Integrated Townships:

1. Palava City: Palava City was developed by the Lodha group and built on a 4500-acre land between Thane, Navi Mumbai and Kalyan. It aims to provide its residents with a sustainable and holistic living experience, offering a mix of residential, commercial, and social infrastructure. The city's development is divided into multiple phases, with several residential neighbourhoods, schools, hospitals, shopping centres, and recreational facilities.

Key Features of Palava City:

1. Infrastructure: Palava City is designed to have a robust infrastructure, including well-planned road networks, efficient water supply and drainage systems, and reliable power supply.
2. Sustainability: The city focuses on sustainability and incorporates various green initiatives. It includes ample green spaces, rainwater harvesting systems, waste management solutions, and energy-efficient buildings.
3. Amenities and Facilities: Palava City offers its residents a range of amenities and facilities. It includes educational institutions, healthcare centres, sports facilities, parks, gardens, community centres, and shopping malls.
4. Connectivity: The city is well-connected to major transportation hubs in Mumbai. Its railway station, called Nilje, provides easy access to other parts of Mumbai and beyond.
5. Smart City Features: The aim of Palava City is to be a smart city by using technology to improve the quality of life for its residents. It includes smart metres, intelligent traffic management systems, and digital infrastructure.
6. Planned Development: The city's development is planned in a phased manner, ensuring that necessary infrastructure and amenities are in place as the population grows.

2. Shantigram: Shantigram is a modern and well-planned residential township on the outskirts of Ahmedabad, Gujarat, India. The property covers an area of 600 acres and is intended to provide a lavish and cosy living experience for its inhabitants. It has various amenities like schools, hospitals, shopping centres, and recreational facilities. It also focuses on sustainability and eco-friendliness, with a sewage treatment plant, rainwater harvesting system, and solar energy to power common areas. This township offers a luxurious lifestyle in a peaceful and eco-friendly environment.

Key Features

1. Luxurious Residences: Shantigram offers a range of residential options, including apartments, penthouses, and villas, catering to different preferences and lifestyles. The residences boast high-quality construction, contemporary architecture, and premium fittings and finishes.

2. Infrastructure and Amenities: The project provides state-of-the-art infrastructure, including well-planned roads, water supply, power distribution, and sewage treatment facilities. Shantigram offers an array of amenities such as schools, hospitals, shopping centres, sports facilities, landscaped gardens, and recreational spaces, ensuring its residents' convenient and enriching lifestyles.

3. Sustainability Initiatives: Shantigram prioritises sustainability and environmental conservation. The project incorporates green building practices, water management systems, and energy-efficient solutions. The township prioritises rainwater harvesting, waste management, and renewable energy sources to decrease its carbon footprint and encourage environmentally friendly lifestyles.

4. Community Development: Shantigram emphasises the development of a strong community spirit. It hosts various cultural and recreational events, promotes social interaction through community centres and clubs, and provides open spaces for residents to engage and connect with each other.

Successes and Impact

1. Premium Living Experience: Adani Shantigram has established itself as a premium residential destination, offering luxury residences with world-class amenities. It has successfully attracted buyers seeking a sophisticated and upscale lifestyle.

2. Economic Growth: The project has contributed to the region's economic growth by generating employment opportunities during the construction phase and creating a market for ancillary services and businesses in the vicinity.

Potential Challenges

1. Timely Execution: Developing a project of this scale requires effective project management and coordination. Ensuring timely execution of construction, infrastructure development, and delivery of amenities can be complex. Most projects are scheduled to be completed between 2025-27.

2. Market Competition: The real estate market in Ahmedabad is competitive, and attracting buyers and investors in a highly competitive market requires offering unique features, quality construction, and a strong value proposition.

3. **Palm Jumeirah:** Palm Jumeirah is a globally renowned and iconic township in Dubai, United Arab Emirates. It is an artificial archipelago developed by Nakheel Properties, one of the leading real estate developers in Dubai.

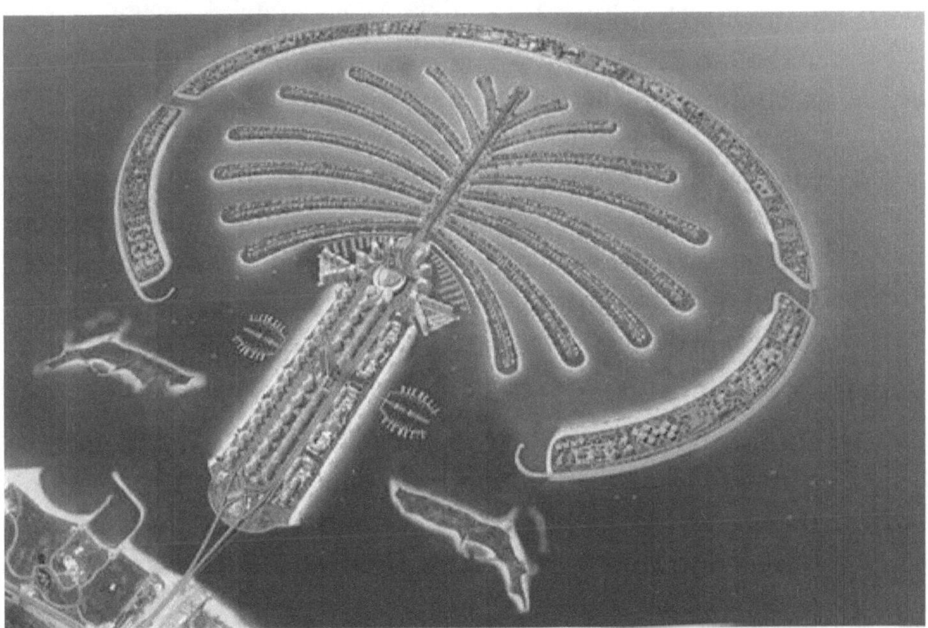

Project Overview

Palm Jumeirah is an artificial island constructed in the shape of a palm tree, extending into the Persian Gulf. The project covers an area of approximately 5 square kilometres and is the first and smallest of the three Palm Islands. Palm Jumeirah offers a mix of residential, commercial, and hospitality developments, making it a highly sought-after destination for luxury living and tourism.

Key Features

1. Luxury Residential Villas and Apartments: Palm Jumeirah features a range of high-end residential options, including luxurious villas and apartments with stunning sea views of the Dubai skyline. The properties are designed to offer exclusive and extravagant living spaces.

2. Iconic Palm-Shaped Design: The unique palm-shaped design of Palm Jumeirah makes it an architectural marvel and a distinctive landmark in Dubai. The island features a crescent-shaped breakwater that acts as a protective barrier against rough seas.

3. World-Class Hotels and Resorts: The township has several renowned hotels and resorts, including Atlantis, The Palm and Jumeirah Zabeel Saray. These establishments offer luxurious accommodations, fine dining experiences, access to private beaches and exclusive amenities.

4. Marina and Waterfront Living: Palm Jumeirah provides residents and visitors access to a vibrant marina and waterfront promenades. The marina offers berthing facilities for yachts, while the waterfront promenades feature restaurants, cafes, and retail outlets, creating a lively and dynamic atmosphere.

Successes and Impact

1. Tourism and Economic Growth: Palm Jumeirah has become a major tourist attraction, attracting visitors from around the world. Luxury hotels, resorts, and entertainment options have contributed to Dubai's tourism industry and overall economic growth.

2. Premium Real Estate Destination: Developing high-end residential properties in Palm Jumeirah has created a niche market for luxury living. The exclusive villas and apartments have become desirable properties for investors and high-net-worth individuals.

3. Landmark Development: Palm Jumeirah has become an internationally recognised symbol of Dubai's architectural and engineering prowess. It has garnered global attention and has made Dubai a destination for luxury and innovation.

Challenges Faced

1. Construction and Engineering: Building an artificial island of this scale requires extensive engineering expertise and innovative construction techniques. The challenges included dredging and reclaiming land from the sea and managing the construction of structures on an unstable seabed.

2. Environmental Considerations: Developing an artificial island had potential ecological impacts, such as disrupting marine ecosystems and altering coastal processes. Ensuring sustainability and minimising ecological damage required careful planning and mitigation measures.

3. Infrastructure Development: Establishing the necessary infrastructure, including transportation networks, utilities, and services, on a remote island presented logistical challenges. It required significant investments in infrastructure development and coordination with various stakeholders.

Chapter 8

Smart Cities

Introduction

A smart city applies information and communication technology to increase operational effectiveness, exchange information with the public, and deliver improved government services and citizen welfare.

A smart city's major objective is to maximise city operations, promote economic development, and enhance citizens' quality of life by utilising smart technology and data analysis. Not just how much technology is accessible but also how it is used determines its worth.

The smartness

- of a city is evaluated based on its technological infrastructure
- environmental initiatives
- efficient public transportation
- forward-thinking city plans
- and the ability of its residents to utilise the city's resources for both living and working.

For a smart city to succeed, it's crucial to establish a strong partnership between the public and private sectors, particularly when it comes to bureaucracy and regulations. Most of the labour required to establish and sustain a digital, data-driven environment is done outside the government. Thus, this partnership is essential.

Smart City Mission

The Smart City Mission is an initiative launched by the Government of India in 2015 to develop 100 cities across the country into smart cities. The aim of the mission is to improve quality of life for residents by using technology and data-driven approaches to enhance infrastructure, services, and sustainability.

Key features and objectives of the Smart City Mission:

1. City selection: The selection of smart cities is based on a competitive process, where cities are chosen based on their proposals and strategies for urban development. Each state in India nominates a certain number of cities, and the Ministry of Housing and Urban Affairs makes the final selection.

2. Smart City Plan: Each selected city prepares a Smart City Proposal (SCP) outlining its vision, goals, and implementation plans for transforming into a smart city. The SCP includes various components such as retrofitting, redevelopment, pan-city initiatives, and a smart city command and control centre.

3. Area-based development: The mission focuses on transforming specific areas within each city, known as Area-Based Development (ABD). These areas are chosen based on their potential for improvement and include initiatives like developing smart infrastructure, affordable housing, public spaces, and sustainable mobility solutions.

4. Pan-city initiatives: In addition to ABD, smart cities also implement pan-city initiatives that leverage technology and data to improve the overall functioning of the city. These initiatives may include projects related to smart governance, e-governance, waste management, energy efficiency, and intelligent transportation systems.

5. Technology integration: The mission emphasises integrating technology and data-driven solutions into urban planning and management. This includes using smart grids, sensor networks, Internet of Things (IoT) devices, data analytics, and other digital tools to enhance efficiency, sustainability, and citizen services.

6. Citizen participation: The Smart City Mission encourages active citizens' involvement in planning and decision-making. Citizens are involved through various mechanisms, such as

public consultations, citizen feedback systems, and citizen-centric service delivery mechanisms.

7. Sustainability and liveability: The mission promotes sustainable development and aims to improve the liveability of cities. This includes initiatives for resource conservation, green infrastructure, eco-friendly transportation, renewable energy, and measures to enhance the quality of life for all residents.

Smart Cities in India

1. NAINA CIDCO, Maharashtra

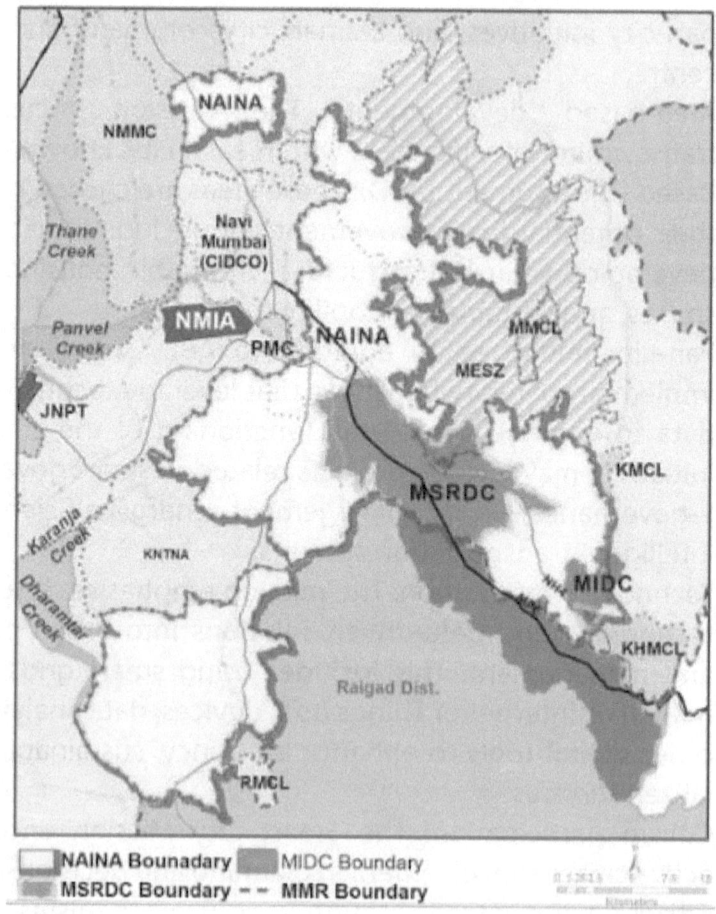

The Navi Mumbai Airport Influence Notified Area (NAINA) CIDCO Smart City is a planned development near the upcoming Navi Mumbai International Airport in Maharashtra, India. It is being developed by CIDCO (City and Industrial Development Corporation), which is the planning authority for Navi Mumbai. NAINA occupies land within a 25-kilometre radius of the airport, roughly 600 square kilometres. The purpose of NAINA is "to avoid unplanned haphazard growth around the proposed airport". The goal of this project is to create a city that is sustainable and includes all essential services such as residential, commercial, and educational facilities. The NAINA CIDCO Smart City aims to attract investment and generate employment opportunities by developing industrial and commercial zones, promoting economic growth.

Development potential of lands in NAINA as per MMR plan:

The project area is classified into Gaothans, areas up to 200m of Gaothan, Special Township Projects, and Rental Housing Projects, segregated by large swathes of lands largely under U1/U2/G1/G2 zones of MMR Plan.

The area of around 200m of each Jonathan has a benefit of 1.0 FSI. Beyond these areas, lands under U1 and U2 zones have base FSI of 0.2 to 0.35, depending upon the sizes of the land holdings.

The lands in G1 and G2 zones have low development potential, with FSI ranging from 0.05 to 0.10 to maintain the environmental character of the area.

Thus as per the MMR plan before CIDCO was appointed as SPA, the development potential available to the landowners needed to be higher, and there needed to be more authority to take up the physical and social infrastructure.

Thus, for example, if anybody has 2000 sq.m of land. As per MMR regulations, the permissible built-up area would be 400 sq.m.

Sr. No	Use	Gaothan	Urban Village	Predominantly Residential	Mixed Use	LDZ	Recreational Zone	Industries & Warehousing
1	2	3	4	5	6	7	8	9
1	NAINA Scheme - Equal to more than 4 ha	1.70 + 0.00	1.70 + 0.00	Not Permissible	Not Permissible	Not Permissible	Not Permissible	Not Permissible
2	NAINA Scheme -Equal to more than 7.5 ha and less than 10 ha	1.70 + 0.00	1.70 + 0.00	2.00 + 0.00	2.00 + 0.00	Not Permissible	Not Permissible	Not Permissible
3	NAINA Scheme -10 ha or more and upto 25 ha	1.70 + 0.00	1.70 + 0.00	1.70 + 0.00	1.70 + 0.00	Not Permissible	Not Permissible	1.70 + 0.00
4	NAINA Scheme - More than 25 ha (20 Ha for LDZ) and upto 40 ha	1.80 + 0.00	1.80 + 0.00	1.80 + 0.00	1.80 + 0.00	1.70 + 0.00	Not Permissible	1.70 + 0.00
5	NAINA Scheme - More than 40 ha	1.90 + 0.00	1.90 + 0.00	1.90 + 0.00	1.90 + 0.00	1.70 + 0.00	Not Permissible	1.70 + 0.00
6	Buildable Amenity as per Regulation No. 13.4.5 for NAINA Scheme	1.70 + 0.00	1.70 + 0.00	2.00 + 0.00	1.70 + 0.00	1.70 + 0.00	Not Permissible	1.70 + 0.00
7	Land contributed under NAINA –Schemes and/or ITP used for purpose other than DP reservations	1.70 + 0.00	1.70 + 0.00	1.70 + 0.00	1.70 + 0.00	1.70 + 0.00	Not Permissible	1.70 + 0.00
8	Buildable Amenity Plots (Reserved in Development Plan)	1.00 + 1.00#	1.00 + 1.00#	1.00 + 1.00#	1.00 + 1.00#	1.00 + 1.00#	1.00 + 1.00#	1.00 + 1.00#
9	Non-Buildable Reservation - For uses ancillary to the main purpose	0.15 + 0.00	0.15 + 0.00	0.15 + 0.00	0.15 + 0.00	0.15 + 0.00	0.15 + 0.00	0.15 + 0.00
10	Growth Centre and Station Area Facility (Reserved in Development Plan)	1.70 + 0.00	1.70 + 0.00	1.70 + 0.00	1.70 + 0.00	1.70 + 0.00	1.70 + 0.00	1.70 + 0.00
11	Theme Based Development	Not Permissible	Not Permissible	Not Permissible	Not Permissible	0.20 + 0.30	Not Permissible	Not Permissible
12	Theme Based Development plan reservations	Not Permissible	Not Permissible	Not Permissible	Not Permissible	1.70 + 0.00	Not Permissible	Not Permissible
13	Other Development	1.00 + 0.00	0.70 + 0.30	0.20 + 0.30	0.20 + 0.30	0.20 + 0.00	0.20 + 0.00	0.50 + 0.50
14	Buildable layout Amenity as per Regulation No. 20.3.11 for other development	1.00 + 0.00	1.00 + 0.00	0.50 + 0.00	0.50 + 0.00	0.20 + 0.00	0.20 + 0.00	1.0 + 0.00
15	NAINA Scheme and Growth Center within 500m buffer as shown in DP	The maximum permissible FSI for such developments is 3.00, on payment of Premium over and above base FSI as explained above.						

(Figure: Maximum Permissible Base FSI + FSI with Payment of premium)

Source: DCPR NAINA 2017

2. Indore

The base FSI for zones Residential, Residential-Commercial & Commercial shall be 1.5.

Road Width (ROW)	Base FSI (as per Indore Development Plan 2021)	Additional FSI (50% TDR* & 50% Premium)
Below 18 m	1.5	As per TDR Policy
18 m	1.5	
24 m	1.5	
30 m	1.5	

If a building proposal was approved before these Regulations were proposed, the owner may use the remaining development rights not exceeding the Total permissible FSI as per these regulations by utilising TDR and paying a premium.

In cases where land is affected by road widening or land acquisition for public purposes, the owner has the right to use TDR as compensation and obtain additional FSI on the same land/building parcel or sell the

FSI as per TDR policy. If TDR is not available through a private owner, the plot owner may choose to avail additional FSI through the FSI premium provided by IMC.

Relaxation in FSI

In the case of units affected by widening of road or construction of a new road, the owner may claim FSI from the Competent Authority as compensation for the surrendered land. In the case of FSI, the Competent Authority shall permit the FSI of any such land/plot or Building-unit based on the original boundary of the Building Unit. Before securing Development Permission on any such Building-units, the owner shall have to surrender the affected land, which shall be calculated as follows:

Compensation as TDR = Surrendered Land (sqm) x Base F.S.I. x 2

3. GIFT City

A true "Walk to Work" city, GIFT City is a planned development covering 886 acres of land and featuring 62 million square feet of built-up area. It offers a variety of spaces, including offices, apartments, schools, hospitals, hotels, clubs, retail outlets, and recreational facilities. The Special Economic Zone (SEZ) of GIFT City comprises a welcoming Multi-Service Area and a privileged Domestic Area. This city will maximise the use of the land area for development because it is a vertical city. The city is situated along the Sabarmati River, which links Gujarat State's political and commercial centres of Ahmedabad and Gandhinagar. Gujarat State is considered to be India's growth engine. A new financial and technological gateway for the world, GIFT City, is located in India. The city allows a maximum of 3.65 FSI.

The first of its type in India, GIFT City, is being built as a centre for global banking and IT/ITES. The urban development of GIFT includes brand-new structures, including resorts, high-rise shopping malls, and apartments. Gujarat International Finance Tech is referred to as GIFT. Its goal is to establish a global financial hub for domestic and international financial services that will be a role model for the upcoming infrastructure, environmental protection, and quality of life improvements. GIFT City will act as the geographic centre of western

India and as an example of equitable, ecologically responsible growth driven by a competitive market economy centred on trade and related industry.

The GIFT Area Plan must be followed for all sorts of city development. At Gift City, integrated development is practised. The Global FSI in the GIFT Area is 3.65 according to the approved GIFT Area Plan. A LEED (Leadership in Energy and Environmental Design) certification is required for any building in the GIFT Area.

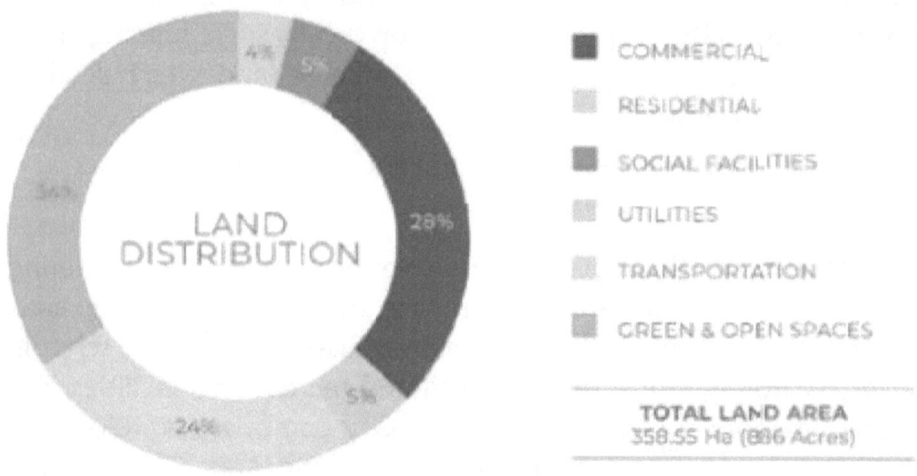

Source - Official Gift City Brochure

Residential land uses include multi-story apartments, studios, serviced apartments, and other such uses as may be specified by the Competent Authority on the suggestion of GIFTCL.

Commercial land uses include offices, financial services, IT/ITeS, retail shopping, business, hotels, restaurants, shopping, cinemas & malls.

The provisions of UDAS (Urban Design and Architectural Sheet) will be followed in placing the coordinates of water supply, drainage, sewerage, solid waste management, power, district cooling, gas, telecommunication, security and surveillance system tapping/ collection sites. The construction plan must include an Intelligent Construction Management System (IBMS). The IBMS will include, but will not be limited to, monitoring and surveillance of utilities, services, safety, security management, fire fighting systems, and other similar systems. IBMS created in this manner must be compatible with the Intelligent urban system envisioned for the GIFT Area and synchronised with the GIFT Area's central control and command centre to the satisfaction of GIFTCL.

Source - GIFT Area Development Control Regulations, October 2011

4. Dholera Special Investment Region

Dholera Special Investment Region is an industrial smart city about 100 kilometres southwest of Ahmedabad. It is intended to be India's most appealing manufacturing and industrial development site. The Gujarat government has built a legislative framework for constructing a Special Investment Region (SIR) under the Act 2009, for which a regional development authority DSIR has been constituted.

There are various land use zones as per the Draft General Development Control Regulations (DGDCR) issued by the DSIRDA.

1. Residential zone
2. High Access Corridor zone
3. City Centre zone

4. Knowledge and IT Zone
5. Industrial Zone
6. Logistic Zone
7. Village Buffer Zone
8. Recreation, Sports and Entertainment Zone
9. Green space
10. Agriculture Zone
11. Solar park Zone
12. Tourism & Resorts
13. Strategic Infrastructure
14. Pubic Facilities Zone

The way the land uses are differentiated shows that the government has done careful planning to ensure that the growth of Dholera City takes place in a sustainable, green, eco-friendly, and citizen-centric way. With these rules, Dholera's development will meet the requirements of all societal groups while being environmentally benign and sustainable. This procedure results in varied government perks and taxes for business owners and producers.

All buildings and structures have to follow these General Development & Building requirements:

1. Sustainability
2. Minimum Plot Sizes
3. Drainage and flood prevention

To ensure sustainability in new construction buildings, it is advised to follow the guidelines set forth by the GRIHA rating system developed by the Ministry of New and Renewable Energy and TERI. These regulations promote environmentally-friendly practices.

The city has excellent connectivity through the various modes of transport.

Draft General Development Control Regulations (DGDCR)

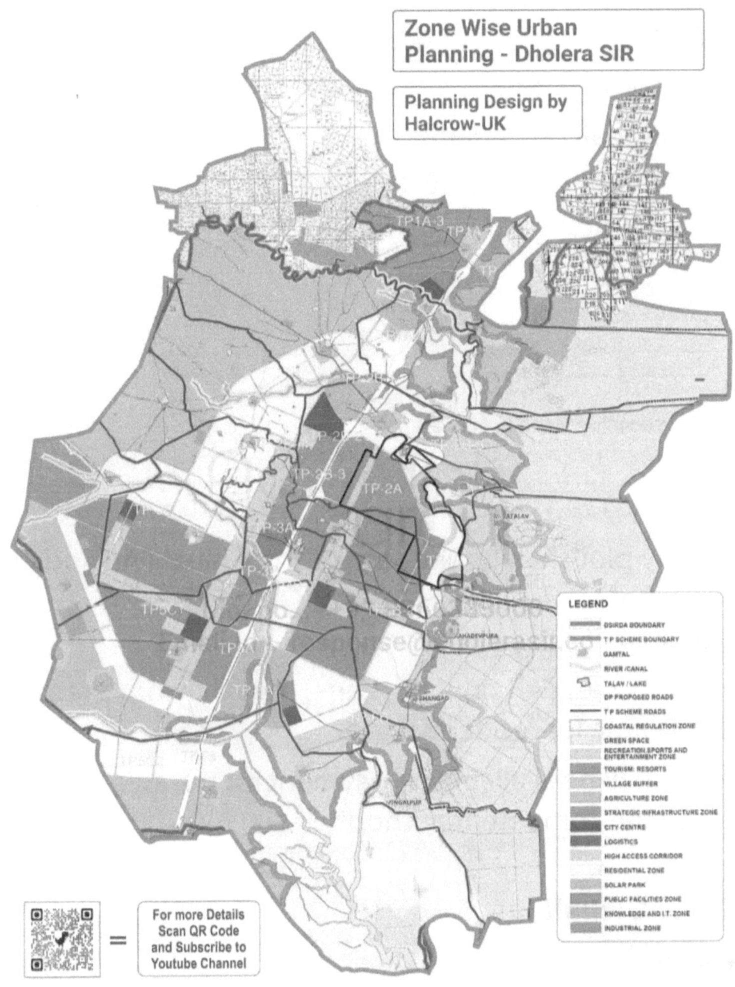

Dholera greenfield smart city | www.dholerasir.co | +91 8866333000

Regulations for residential township

Maximum permissible use FAR- 1.5

Total FAR permitted on Gross plot area and shall be the sum of Global FAR and Additional FAR as under

i. Global FAR (GFAR) shall be 1.0

ii. Additional premium FAR shall be permitted on payment to DSIRDA,

Additional FAR	Premium Rates
25% of GFAR	Additional 40% of the Jantri Rates
Additional 25% of GFAR	Additional 50% of the Jantri Rates

Maximum FAR shall be under: -

MIN ROAD ROW (M)	MIN. PLOT SIZE	MAX FAR	MAX GROUND COVERAGE	MAX HEIGHT* (M)	MINIMUM SETBACKS (FRONT-REAR-BOTH SIDES)
55m & above	5000 sqm**	5	0-10%	150m	10m-8m-6m-6m
		4	Above 10-20%	126m	9m-7m-6m-6m
		3	Above 20-30%	32m	8m-6m-6m-6m
25m & Below 55	1500 sqm	2.5	40%	20m	8m-6m-6m-6m
Below 25m	1500 sqm	2	40%	16m	8m-6m-6m-6m

** For Plot sizes of 5000 sqm and above – In case of a building with podium and tower, a ground coverage of maximum 40% will be allowed for a maximum height upto 8 m, including G or G+1 whichever is less. The upper typical floors above podium will have a maximum plan area of 10%. The maximum FAR allowed in this case will be 5.

The FSI on any plot shall be the sum of the Global FAR and Premium FSI where Global FSI

- o 0.6 in any area or
- o Permissible FAR in any zone, not having premium and applicable for residential use.

Premium FSI shall be available on payment for the area at 40% of land jantri rates to the competent authority.

Smart Cities Globally

1. Singapore

Narendra Modi, the Prime Minister of India, admires Singapore's achievement in constructing affordable homes for its expanding population. According to Bloomberg, a typical 100 square metre house in Singapore would require 42 years of an average citizen's income, whereas in Mumbai, India's financial hub, it would take 308 years. Singapore has been successful in building affordable homes while avoiding overcrowding. Despite being the third-densest country in the world, Singapore's population grew from 1.6 million to 5.4 million between 1960 and 2015, yet it still managed to become less crowded.

The success of Singapore is evident from the fact that Andhra Pradesh Chief Minister Chandrababu Naidu has decided to model the state's new capital Amaravati in Singapore. Singaporean company Surbana Jurong will help the southern state in implementing this model.

Listed below are a few lessons from Singapore's success that our government's Housing for All mission can rely on:

- Singapore is a small country spanning across 710 square kilometres. Despite its size, the country has experienced high levels of immigration due to its open policies. This has led to an increase in real estate prices. However, Singapore has been able to effectively manage its growing population by allowing high building density. Through this approach, the city-state has been able to create more floor space on limited land, with a floor space index (FSI) of 25 in the central business district (CBD).

- Data shows that Singapore's annual GDP per capita is $56,287, while India's is $1,596. This is another reason why citizens of Singapore find homes more affordable. In a country like Singapore, where land is scarce, homes can be made affordable only by using capital instead of land. This means homes can be cheaper if greater floor space is built on existing land.

- Singapore has developed world class transportation networks, ports, and airports. Better infrastructure networks have made more urban land accessible to the public. Building bridges around the bay has also made greater land available by linking land masses that are not contiguous. Cities like Mumbai have the same geographical constraints and have yet to do this. This has made homes more affordable in Singapore, where the percentage of home ownership is among the highest all over the world.

2. New York, USA

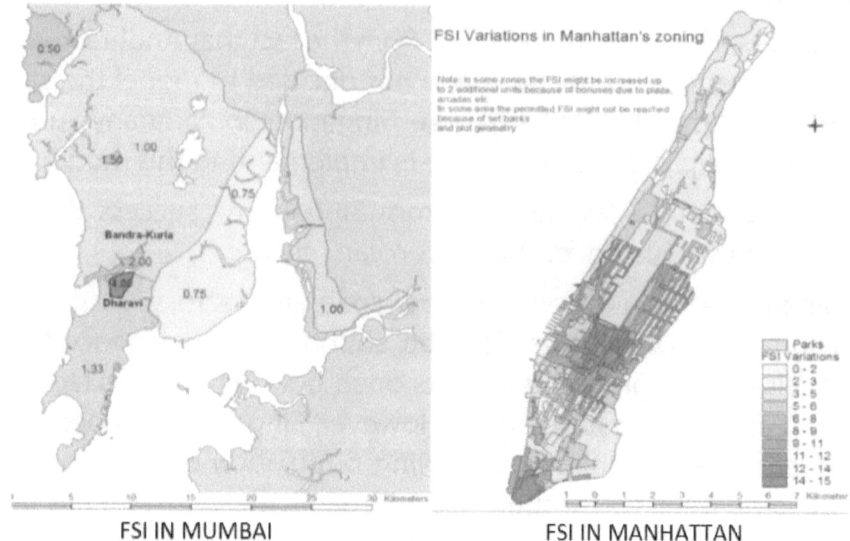

FSI IN MUMBAI   FSI IN MANHATTAN

- The above images compare the Floor Space Index (FSI) in Mumbai and Manhattan, New York City. FSI is largely uniform across Mumbai. It is neither differentiated between commercial and residential areas nor linked to land market values. Additionally, although higher FSI near transit nodes enables easy access to transport, Mumbai's FSI does not increase closer to the transit nodes.

- In contrast, Manhattan's Floor Space Index (FSI) varies more depending on economic activity. This leads to a higher FSI in the city centre, particularly in the central business district (CBD), and a lower FSI as you move further away from it. This higher FSI in CBDs with limited land available allows for taller buildings and less urban sprawl, enabling people to live closer to their workplaces.

- FSI limits were initially implemented to control urbanisation and limit densification, but they have had the opposite effect. Instead of benefiting cities and promoting growth, uniform FSI limits have restricted the availability of developable land, driving up land prices and the cost of living in urban areas.

3. Dubai

Dubai's distinct FSI strategy allows for multi-story construction in certain locations while maintaining open spaces and measuring development and sustainability. The FSI constraints imposed by Dubai have permitted the building of enormous projects such as the world's highest skyscraper, the Burj Khalifa.

Dubai's smart city strategy comprises more than a hundred initiatives and a proposal to transform 1,000 government services into smart services. The project aims to stimulate collaboration between the public and commercial sectors to achieve goals in six 'smart' priority areas: smart life, smart transit, smart society, smart economy, smart governance, and smart environment. Three fundamental ideas underpin the strategy: communication, integration, and cooperation.

According to the Green Building Council (GBC), the UAE ranks ninth globally in terms of the total area of space certified to LEED (Leadership in Energy and Environmental Design) standards. LEED certification is awarded to buildings based on their cost efficiency and energy-saving capabilities. The energy consumption of buildings is a major community issue in the UAE. The Dubai Municipality introduced a set of standards in 2010 that encourages using energy-saving devices, natural lighting systems, and green building materials. Dubai's Integrated Energy Strategy has a lofty goal of lowering energy and water usage by 30% by 2030. The DEWA (Dubai Electricity and Water Authority) and Dubai Municipality are working hard to reduce building cooling requirements.

Sustainable Design - Dubai's smart city plans prioritise sustainability, and FSI legislation helps to promote environmentally friendly design practices. Higher density in specific areas can encourage successful public transport networks, shorten travel times, and reduce carbon emissions.

High-Density Development - Dubai's FSI rules allow for high-density development in specific zones, particularly in the central business district and significant commercial sectors. This approach promotes vertical expansion and maximises land use efficiency, contributing to the city's overall smart urban planning goal.

The 'Dubai Urban Area Strategic Plan' outlines goals for urban development, including expanding land for residential, industrial, and commercial use, improving transportation, and promoting economic growth.

4. Shenzhen, China

Over the course of 40 years, Shenzhen has transformed from a small fishing village into a bustling international metropolis. It has earned the titles of 'China's Silicon Valley' and 'China's smartest city'.

The ambition to make it a world-class city has characterised the planning documents since the 1990s. Three main phases of urban planning in Shenzhen: the 1980-85 period, the 1985-90 period and the post-1990 period. Three urban master plans describe the shaping of land use from a clustered linear model to a multiple axes network structure and then towards a polycentric urban development model with two centres and five sub-centres

In the latest version of the Shenzhen Urban Planning Standards and Guidelines (2014), the land-use classification includes nine main categories and 31 subcategories. The nine main categories include residential land (R), commercial and service facility land (C), government and community land (GIC), industrial land (M), Waterhouse land (W), roads and squares (S), municipal utilities (U), green spaces (G), and water bodies and another non-urban development land (E).

The Urban Planning and Land Resources Commission of Shenzhen Municipality, also known as the Shenzhen Planning Bureau (SPB), is responsible for managing land use regulations and urban planning.

Conclusion

Foreign smart cities have tried to maintain the affordability of housing by allowing more FSI in the Central Business Districts. The area near the CB has grown vertically with high property prices, and the middle-income group can afford areas far from the CBD. Foreign countries have linked the permissible FSI to the economic activity within the area so that people can reach their workplaces early. On the other hand, FSI has been uniform throughout the Island city and suburbs, causing an increase in housing prices drastically. If such cities are turned into smart cities, the prices of the properties will increase even more. Since India is a developing country, we should focus on affordable housing. Turning cities smart is the need of the hour, but also the regulations of the FSI should be revised so that the prices remain within reach of the middle-income group.

FSI and Environment (ESG)

Environmental, Social and Governance

Environmental, Social, and Governance (ESG) has become an essential idea in the worldwide real estate sector, including in India. Real estate developers and investors progressively incorporate environmental, social, and governance aspects into their decision-making processes, recognising the importance of sustainability, social responsibility, and ethical governance in real estate development and investment.

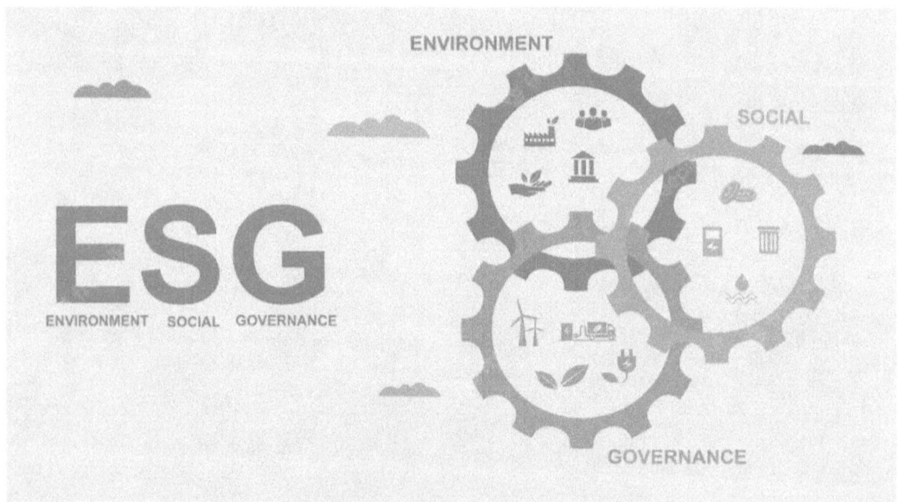

Important terms related to the environment

1. Reserve Forest: Reserve forests are areas of protected forest that the government legally manages for conservation. They were established in India under the Indian Forest Act of 1927, which regulates the protection and management of the country's forests and wildlife. Forest departments of the states manage forest reserves and are responsible for controlling access to and use of forest resources. Hunting, mining and grazing are generally prohibited in the reserve, but research and ecotourism are permitted under certain conditions.

2. NDZ: No-Development Zone (NDZ) is an area of land designated for a specific purpose and unsuitable for construction. NDZs are often sensitive areas or have significant constraints that make them unsuitable for development. NDZs are usually defined by Indian state or local governments and can be found in urban, suburban or rural areas.

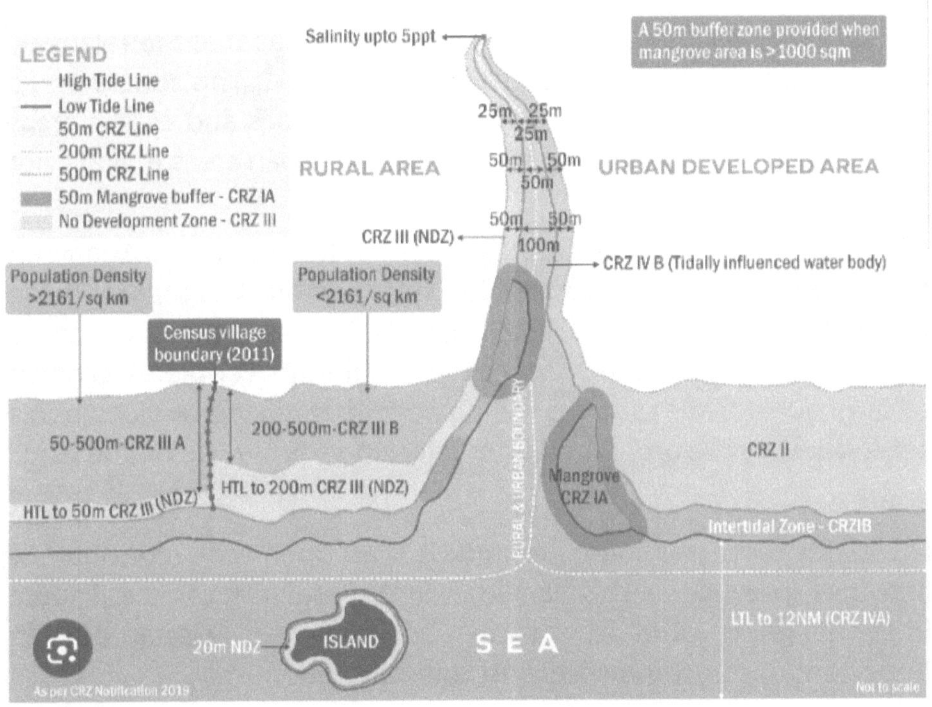

3. CRZ: The Coastal Regulation Zones (CRZ) refer to the regions along India's extensive 7,500 km coastline. The official notification defines the Coastal Regulation Zone as the coastal land that extends up to 500m from the High Tide Line (HTL), as well as a stretch of 100m along the banks of creeks, backwaters, estuaries, and rivers that are affected by tidal fluctuations. The Government of India regulates the development of buildings, tourist spots, and other facilities in these areas.

CRZ-1: These are ecologically sensitive areas essential in maintaining the ecosystem of the coasts. These include national parks, marine parks, reserve forests, sanctuaries, wildlife habitats, mangroves and coral reefs. These areas are situated between the high and low tide lines.

CRZ-2: This zone includes the areas that have been developed up to the shoreline of the coast. It is prohibited to construct unauthorised structures in this zone.

CRZ-3: CRZ-3 encompasses rural and urban areas that are relatively untouched and not categorised as CRZ-1 or CRZ-2. This zone permits only certain agriculture or public facility activities and covers areas within municipal limits or legally designated urban areas that are not heavily developed.

CRZ-4: CRZ-4 includes the coastal regions of Lakshadweep, Andaman and Nicobar Islands, and some other smaller islands, except for those that are classified as CRZ-1, CRZ-2, or CRZ-3. These areas are located within the aquatic region up to the territorial limits. People are allowed to carry out activities such as fishing and other related services in this zone, but they are prohibited from releasing solid waste on the land.

4. RG

RG stands for recreational grounds. It is an open space for outdoor activities in a large urban environment. Residents can participate in sports, games, and other recreational activities. RGs can play an important role in community and cultural events.

Regulations affecting the development and FSI restrictions across India (Covered in Residential and Commercial FSI)

Regulations affecting the development and FSI restrictions across the globe

1. **Singapore:** FSI regulations in Singapore are applied based on the land use zone and the maximum height of the building. The limits are intended to balance the necessity for growth and protecting green places and the environment.

The government has also created different incentives to encourage sustainable development, such as greater FSI for developments with green elements or that incorporate public areas.

2. **UK**: Building FSI in the UK is limited by planning regulations, but these restrictions vary depending on the area and type of development. In London, for example, the maximum FSI is normally 1.5. However, this may be increased in boom zones. The FSI may be higher in different parts of the UK.

3. **The United States:** FSI restrictions are enforced by municipal governments in the United States, and they vary greatly across the country. In New York City, for example, the FSI is regulated at 12 in specific regions, whereas in San Francisco, the FSI is normally capped at 8.

4. **China:** The central government imposes FSI regulations in China, which vary based on the location and kind of development. For example, the FSI is normally restricted at 3.0 in Shanghai, but this may be increased in certain boom regions.

5. **Dubai:** The Dubai Municipality imposes FSI regulations in Dubai, which vary depending on the location and kind of development. For example, the FSI in the central business area is normally regulated at 5.0, although it may be greater in other parts of the city.

Countries across the globe which have considered environmental regulations in the development of cities

1. **Dubai:** Dubai has grown into a significant economic and tourism centre while simultaneously taking steps to address environmental problems. For example, the city has enacted various laws to promote sustainable development, such as legislation mandating developers to incorporate green spaces and utilise energy-efficient materials in construction. Dubai has also significantly invested in renewable energy sources such as solar power and has implemented initiatives to enhance air quality.

2. **The United Kingdom:** There is a considerable emphasis in the United Kingdom on balancing the need for development with the preservation of cultural heritage and environmental concerns. The country has implemented several laws encouraging sustainable growth, such as regulations to minimise carbon emissions, promote renewable energy sources, and safeguard green spaces. Furthermore, many cities in the United Kingdom have implemented urban planning policies that prioritise pedestrian and bike-friendly transportation options, reducing reliance on automobiles and promoting sustainable living.

3. **The United States:** While environmental legislations differ by state, several cities have created policies to address environmental concerns. New York City, for example, has enacted several regulations to minimise carbon emissions, promote renewable energy sources, and reduce waste. San Francisco has also put in place a number of measures aimed at lowering the city's carbon footprint and enhancing air and water quality.

4. **China:** In recent years, China has taken major strides to address environmental concerns, including enacting air and water pollution rules, supporting renewable energy sources, and decreasing trash. In addition, the country has implemented a number of efforts to promote sustainable development, such as green building programmes and urban planning rules that prioritise green space and public transit.

Many cities worldwide have put in place various policies and measures to address environmental problems while supporting sustainable growth. These policies frequently seek to minimise carbon emissions, encourage renewable energy, protect green spaces, and reduce waste.

Case Studies Related to Violation of environmental norms

1. Sanjay Gandhi National Park: Sanjay Gandhi National Park, like many other protected areas in India, has faced challenges related to **encroachment** and unauthorised activities within its boundaries. Encroachment refers to the illegal occupation or use of land within the park, which can significantly negatively impact its ecosystems and wildlife. Here are some key points regarding encroachment in Sanjay Gandhi National Park:

- Informal Settlements: One of the major encroachment issues in the park is the presence of informal settlements or slums within its boundaries. Over the years, people have established illegal dwellings, often constructed haphazardly, leading to encroachment on park land.

- Tribal Villages: Sanjay Gandhi National Park is also home to tribal communities like the Warli tribe. While these communities have been residing in the area for generations, some of their settlements may be considered encroachments under the legal framework due to the park's protected status.

- Farming and Agriculture: Encroachment for agricultural purposes is another concern within the park. Some individuals have engaged in farming by clearing land and cultivating crops illegally within the park's boundaries.

- Quarrying and Mining: Encroachment by illegal quarrying and mining activities has also been reported in and around the park. Such activities can destroy habitats, soil erosion, and other ecological damage.

- Wildlife Trafficking: Encroachment can facilitate illegal activities like wildlife trafficking. The park's diverse wildlife, including leopards, can be targeted by poachers who encroach on the park to carry out their activities.

- Eviction and Rehabilitation: Authorities have periodically conducted eviction drives to remove encroachments and illegal structures within the park. In some cases, alternative housing or rehabilitation measures have been undertaken to provide affected individuals with alternative settlements.

Encroachment poses a significant threat to the ecological integrity and conservation efforts of Sanjay Gandhi National Park. Park authorities, the forest department, and conservation organisations have made efforts to address the issue through eviction drives, public awareness campaigns, and community participation in conservation initiatives. However, encroachment remains a persistent challenge that requires ongoing vigilance and concerted efforts to protect and preserve the park's valuable ecosystems and wildlife. Over 25 years have passed since the High Court ordered the removal of encroachment, but little has changed. The number of hutments has risen, and now Sai Bangoda near Vihar Lake has also been affected. Almost 100 acres of forest land have been illegally occupied.

2. Maradu Apartment Demolition Case: The Maradu Apartment Complex in Kerala, consisting of four luxury waterfront apartments, was constructed in **violation of CRZ regulations**, which allowed construction only beyond 200 metres of the high tide line. The apartment complex's location fell under CRZ-III, classified as a No Development Zone (NDZ). According to CRZ regulations, no construction is permitted in such areas to protect the coastal environment and prevent unauthorised development.

A PIL (public interest litigation) was filed in the Kerala High Court, highlighting the CRZ violations by the Maradu Apartment Complex. The court took cognisance of the matter and initiated legal proceedings. The builders also ignored the show cause notice given by the Maradu Panchayat.

But after a long legal battle, the fate of the high-rise buildings -- H20 Holy Faith, Alfa Serene, Jain Coral Cove and Golden Kayaloram -- in Kerala's Maradu was sealed after a 2019 Supreme Court order. Eviction notices were served to the residents.

So by the 12th of January, all four high-rise buildings were demolished as they violated CRZ regulations.

Way Forward for India

1. Green Buildings: India provides limited incentives for environmentally friendly construction. An environmental performance assessment method for buildings is offered by the Indian Green Building Council (IGBC), known as the Green Assessment for Integrated Habitat Assessment (GRIHA). But only government structures and public utilities generally offer rewards for receiving higher ratings. Incentives for promoting green buildings are also offered financially by the Ministry of Housing and Urban Affairs (MoHUA) through various programmes. However, they are rather modest. The Green Mark scheme of Singapore provides tax breaks, subsidies and rebates to producers and owners with higher Green Mark scores. The National Australian Built Environment Rating System (NABERS) of Australia offers incentives such as tax credits and rebates to building owners with higher NABERS ratings. Following the Energy Policy Act of 2005,

the US offers tax credits and subsidies to building owners with higher LEED ratings.

2. Net zero energy building: A zero-energy construction (ZNE) is a building with zero net power consumption, which means that the total annual energy consumption in the building is approximately the same as the amount of renewable energy produced.

3. Efficient Infrastructure: FSI guidelines can include provisions for efficient infrastructure systems, such as water supply, sewage treatment, and waste management. Promoting the use of energy-efficient technologies, encouraging recycling and waste reduction practices, and integrating sustainable stormwater management techniques can minimise the environmental impact of development.

4. Preservation of Cultural and Historical Heritage: While not directly related to environmental sustainability, preserving cultural and historical heritage within FSI guidelines can contribute to sustainable development. Rehabilitating and repurposing existing buildings reduces demolition waste and maintains a place's unique character and identity, fostering a sense of community and reducing the need for new construction.

5. Public Transportation and Connectivity: FSI guidelines can incentivise the provision of efficient public transportation systems and promote connectivity within and between neighbourhoods. By prioritising pedestrian-friendly infrastructure, cycling lanes, and accessible public transportation networks, the reliance on private vehicles can be reduced, leading to lower carbon emissions and improved air quality.

Chapter 10

Redevelopment

Redevelopment refers to revitalising or improving an existing property, area, or infrastructure to enhance its functionality, appearance, or value. It typically involves significant changes and upgrades to outdated, deteriorated, or underutilised spaces to meet the evolving needs of a community or to align with new economic, social, or environmental goals.

Redevelopment may involve renovating or refurbishing existing structures, demolishing old buildings and constructing new ones, or repurposing an area for different use. Redevelopment initiatives are commonly undertaken in urban areas to revitalise neighbourhoods, improve housing conditions, enhance public spaces, or attract investment.

The redevelopment process typically involves extensive planning, coordination, and collaboration among various stakeholders, including government authorities, urban planners, architects, developers, community organisations, and residents. The objectives of redevelopment projects often include upgrading the built environment, promoting economic growth, creating jobs, increasing property values, improving infrastructure, fostering social inclusion, and achieving sustainable development.

In this chapter we will focus mainly on the redevelopment schemes and policies in Mumbai and surrounding areas making up for Mumbai Metropolitan Region

Stages of Redevelopment in Mumbai:

The redevelopment process generally falls into twelve basic phases.

1. Offer Letter to the Society
2. Terms and Conditions with the Society
3. Agreement with the Society
4. Sanction from MCGM in favour of the Society
5. TDR loaded in the Society name
6. Obtaining the IOD
7. Shifting of the members
8. Demolition of the building
9. Obtaining the CC
10. Construction of the New Building
11. Obtaining the OC and BCC
12. Moving the Old members.

Regulation for Redevelopment of Building in CIDCO

Total Permissible Area computation:

Sr. No.	Category	Permissible F.S.I.
1	Plot area 1000 sq.m. or more having Access road minimum 15.0 m width	2.50
2	Plot area 1000 sq.m. or more having Access road minimum 9.0 m width	2.00
3	Any other plot having Access road below 9.0 m width	1.80 or Authorizedly consumed FSI + 50% Incentive – whichever is less

Following components add to permissible area for redevelopment: (if not done by CIDCO)

1. Rehabilitation Entitlement Area:

   To determine the Rehabilitation Area for an existing residential building, the Basic Entitlement Area and the Additional Entitlement Area are merged.

2. Incentive F.S.I.

    Shall be admissible against F.S.I. required for rehabilitation based on Basic Ratio

3. Balance F.S.I.

    The F.S.I. remaining balance after providing for Rehabilitation and Incentive components.

A. REHABILITATION ENTITLEMENT AREA:

The sum of the following:

a. Basic Entitlement Area: The new area will be as big as the current living space plus an additional 35%, but it must be at least 300 square feet.

b. Additional Entitlement Area: Shall be governed by the size of the Plot under Redevelopment as follows:

Area of Plot under Redevelopment	Additional Entitlement (As % of the Carpet area of Existing Tenement)
Upto 4000.0 sq.m.	NIL
Above 4000.0 sq.m. to 2.0 Ha.	10%
Above 2.0 Ha. to 5.0 Ha.	15%
Above 5.0 Ha. To 10.0 Ha.	20%

- The entire parcel of land on which the renovation of hazardous or dilapidated structures is to be done is the "plot under renovation."
- The maximum entitlement area must not exceed the maximum carpet area allowed for the MIG Category as the government approved the redevelopment project.
- The area of the balcony is not included in the Rehabilitation Area Entitlement.
- The Carpet Area of the Existing Unit + 20% Thereof shall constitute the Entitlement of Rehabilitation Area for any Existing Authorised Commercial Unit or Amenity Unit in the Residential Scheme.

B. INCENTIVE FSI:

- NMMC must distribute F.S.I. on the Plot Under Redevelopment, with CIDCO's prior approval. If more than one land rate applies to various areas of the Plot Under Redevelopment, a weighted average must be considered when calculating the Average Land rate and Basic Ratio.

- The year the Redevelopment Project is approved shall be considered when determining the Land and Construction rates.

C. SHARING OF BALANCE FSI:

After paying for rehabilitation and incentive components, any F.S.I. that is left over must be split between CIDCO and any current or projected C.H.S. or Apartment Ownership Association in the form of the built-up area as follows:

Basic Ratio (LR/RC)	Sharing of Balance F.S.I.	
	Society/ Association Share	CIDCO Share
Above 3.00	30%	70%
Above 2.00 and up to 3.00	40%	60%
Above 1.00 and up to 2.00	50%	50%
Up to 1.00	60%	40%

Out of the share of CIDCO, 20% shall be handed over to the Navi Mumbai Municipal Corporation in the form of tenements.

FSI: Redevelopment (MMR)

- DC Regulation 33 of DCPR 2034 deals with additional FSI in certain categories at par with D.C Reg. 33 of DCR 1991.

    1. 33(5): For MHADA Buildings
    2. 33(7): For Cess Category Buildings

        33(7) A: For non- cess tenanted buildings in city and suburbs

        33(7) B: Additional incentive FSI for the redevelopment of existing housing society excluding cessed building

    3. 33(9): For Buildings under the cluster development scheme
    4. 33(10): For slum dwellers
    5. 33(11): Permanent Transit Camps

33(5) For Maharashtra Housing and Area Development Authority (MHADA)

- **This applies to the construction or renovation of residential projects on MHADA-owned land intended for Economically Weaker Sections (EWS), Low-Income Groups (LIG), and Middle-Income Groups (MIG) housing** categories.
- FSI permissible on **gross plot area = 3**
- FSI is permitted to Plot an area of more than **4000 Sq.mt = 4** and fronting road width of more than **18 Mts.**
- Each resident shall be given the **existing carpet area + 35% basic** entitlement subject to **a minimum of 35 Sq.mt.** (376 Sq.ft.)
- For Fungible FSI, rehab building free of premium is available
- For a plot of area up to **4000 Sq.mt. MHADA** may allow payment of premium instead of Constructing and handing over its share.
- In the case of a plot having an area **of 4000 sq. m** or above and a road width of 18 mt. or more, the **FSI 1.00 out of 4 FSI** shall be permissible in the form of Social Housing stock in the **ratio of 1 MHADA: 0.5 Co-operative Society (2/3rd: 1/3rd)**, and it shall be handed over to MHADA free of cost & without any compensation.

33(7) For Cessed Building in the Island City

- Co-operative housing societies may reconstruct or redevelop cessed buildings in the island city, as well as old buildings owned by the corporation, existing prior to 30/06/1969
- 3 FSI on gross plot **OR** Rehab BUA + Incentive, whichever is more.
- Each occupant shall receive a carpet area that ranges from a minimum of 300 Sq.ft. to a maximum of 1292 Sq.ft. The non-residential occupier carpet to be provided shall be equivalent to the area occupied in the old building.

33(7) A: For Tenanted Occupied building

- Applicable to Dilapidated authorised tenanted building/s in Suburbs and Dilapidated authorised Non cessed Tenanted building/s in Island City
- Rehab area + Incentive **OR** Permissible FSI as per Table 12 of regulation 30(A)(1), whichever is more.

- Any tenancy that was created after 13/6/96 will not be taken into consideration.

33(7) B For Residential Housing Societies

- For Housing Societies in Island Cities and Suburbs, which are 30 years old, excluding buildings covered under regulations 33(7) and 33(7)(A):
- Existing area + Incentive **OR** Permissible FSI as per Table no 12 of regulation 30(A)(1), whichever is more.
- 15% Incentive on the Existing authorised area or 10 Sq.mt. Per residential tenement, whichever is more.
- If tenanted building/s and building/s of co-operative housing society/non-tenanted building(s) coexist on the plot under development, then the rules of 33(7)(A) & 33(7)(B) can be combined.

33(9) For Building under Cluster Redevelopment Scheme (CDS)

- Redevelopment of Clusters. Minimum Plot area of 4000 Sq.mt. in Island City and 6000 Sq.mt. in Mumbai & Extended Suburbs. Road width must be 18 mts. wide or more.
- Cessed Buildings, Non-cessed buildings which are 30 years old, and Slums of up to 50% of the area are allowable under Cluster redevelopment.
- 4 FSI **OR** Rehab Built-up area + incentive, whichever is more.

Some Important Sub-sections of CDS are given below:

33(9)(3) Land Pooling: If a public authority approves land pooling for a CDS project and provides compensation, the Municipal Commissioner can make a decision on the proposal without referring it to the empower committee. This applies to proposals that fall under section 33(9)(3).

33(9)(5a): The minimum area for a residential tenement in cluster development for NR has been increased from 27.88 sq.m to 35 sq.m. However, the minimum area remains the same as per existing regulations for other purposes.

33(9)(6b): Incentive:

Earlier- applicable in CRZ

per the Table-B below:

Table-B

Basic Ratio (LR/RC)	Incentive (As % of Admissible Rehabilitation Area)			
	For 0.4ha up to 1 ha	More than 1 ha upto 5ha	More than 5 ha up to 10 ha.	For more than 10 ha
Above 6.00	55%	60%	65%	70%
Above 4.00 and upto 6.00	65%	70%	75%	80%
Above 2.00 and upto 4.00	75%	80%	85%	90%
Upto 2.00	85%	90%	95%	100%

Now proposed for non CRZ area

Table-B

Basic Ratio (LR/RC) (LR/RC)	Incentive (As % of Admissible Rehabilitation Area)			
	For 0.4ha up to 1 ha	More than 1 ha upto 5ha	More than 5 ha up to 10 ha.	For more than 10ha.
Above 6.00	85%	90%	95%	100%
Above 4.00 and upto 6.00	95%	100%	105%	110%
Above 2.00 and upto 4.00	105%	110%	115%	120%
Upto 2.00	115%	120%	125%	130%

33(9)(9): Up to 30% of the incentive FSI can be utilised for non-residential purposes, as allowed by the DCPR. With the approval of the Municipal Commissioner, this percentage can be increased to 50%.

33(9)(13.4): CD plot abuts a DP Road having width of 18.3 m and above. The front marginal open space shall not be insisted upon beyond 3.0 m provided such road is not an Express Highway or a road wider than 52 m.

33(10) For Slum Dwellers

1. **For the** Slum Rehabilitation areas declared or notified under Slum Act.
2. 4 FSI **OR** Rehab Built-up area + incentive, whichever is more.
3. Each rehab tenement shall be given 300 Sq.ft. carpet area
4. A separate Slum Rehabilitation Authority sanctions schemes under the redevelopment of Slum areas.
5. The no. of hutment dwellers is certified by SRA.
6. The density in the SRA scheme is high; hence various relaxations in open spaces are given in SRA schemes.

33(11) PTC of SRA Scheme

This provision allows for the construction of Permanent Transit Camps (PTCs) to rehabilitate slum dwellers.

1. Under the SRA scheme, slum rehabilitation projects are undertaken to upgrade living conditions of the slum dwellers by providing them with permanent housing. The transit camps are temporary accommodations provided to the slum dwellers during the construction of the rehabilitation projects. Once the rehabilitation projects are completed, the slum dwellers are shifted from the transit camps to the new permanent housing units.

2. These transit camps serve as interim housing for slum dwellers and are equipped with basic amenities such as water supply, sanitation facilities, electricity, etc. The purpose of these camps is to ensure that the slum dwellers have a place to live during the construction phase of the rehabilitation projects.

3. Developers can combine plots owned by single or multiple owners to offer a permanent transit component on a single plot. They must shift the sale component and base FSI of the plot to other plots with the agreement of all right holders. Clubbing can only be allowed if it results in an independent plot, building, or wing, with the permanent transit camp component being handed over to the Planning Authority. Additionally, developers must pay an unearned income equal to 40% of the difference in the sale value of the shifted B.U.A of the Permanent Transit Camp component, as per ASR. This clubbing can be allowed within a distance of 5 km.

4. FSI is linked to road width and plot area. Plot area up to 2000 sqm and abutting 12m road width (min) shall get FSI up to 3. Plots of size more than 2000 sqm and abutting 18m road width (min) shall get FSI up to 4.

5. 25% of basic FSI has to be used for shops along layout roads.

DIFFERENCE BETWEEN THE REQULATIONS:

	REG. 30	REG. 33(7)(A)	REG. 33(7)(B)	REG.33(11)
1) ROAD WIDTH	13.20 MT	13.20 MT	13.20 MT	13.20 MT
2) F.S.I PREMISSIBLE	2.20	2.20	2.20	3.00
3) T.D.R COMPONENT	0.70	0.70 – (50% Incentive over rehab area)	0.70 – (15% of Existing BUA or 10 sq.m per tenement)	NO TDR
4) 50% GOVT F.S.I	0.50	0.50	0.50	1.00

Calculation of FSI and scheme parameters:-

Sr. No.	Description	Non-slum plot under Regulation 33(11) of DCP-2034.			
1.	Gross area of scheme plot considered for the scheme	1602.10			
2.	Deduction for D.P. Reservations i) Road setback ii) existing bldg. area (421.63+0.97) =	i) 8.13 ii) 422.60			
3.	Balance Area of plot adopted for the scheme	1171.37			
4.	Deduction for 15% RG (if applicable)	Nil			
5.	Net area of plot (3-4)	1171.37			
6.	Addition for FSI purpose 100% of (2) above	Nil			
7.	Total plot area for FSI purpose	1171.37			
8.	In-situ FSI permissible on plot	4.00			
9.	Total in-situ BUA permissible on plot (7 x 8)	4685.48			
10.	Permissible BUA as per regulation 33(11)	Zonal FSI	PTC	Free Sale	Total
		1171.37	1748.925	1748.925	4669.22
11.	Road set-back area added for 2 times for sale i.e. [2(i) x 2]	16.26	--	--	16.26
12.	Total permissible BUA	1187.63	1748.925	1748.925	4685.48
13.	Total BUA proposed for the Scheme	1187.63	1537.32	1537.32	4262.27
14.	Total FSI consumed for the scheme	1.01	1.31	1.31	3.63
15.	PTC tenements proposed	48 Nos.			

(example taken for understanding purposes)

DCPR 33(12)(B)

Removal and re-accommodation of tolerated /protected structures falling in the alignment of road.

This scheme has been proposed to quickly remove obstacles in the way of existing roads or widen them by relocating protected buildings within the same administrative ward. In this scheme, it may be permissible to exceed the allowable FSI.

To determine eligibility for occupancy of non-cess structures, the Assistant Commissioner of the respective ward and MHADA must certify the existence of the structure on site, the carpet area of the structures, and the eligibility of the occupants. For cessed structures, MHADA must also provide certification.

It is allowed to develop plots under combination of various regulations, but the maximum FSI on a plot cannot exceed the limit set by the respective regulations. For instance, in the case of 33(12)B, the maximum FSI on the net plot is 4.00, whereas in the case of 33(7), the maximum FSI on the gross plot is 3.0 and 1.0 on the net plot.

Combination scheme 33(12) B with any other than 33(7)			Combination scheme 33(12) B with 33(7)		
Sr.no	Description	Area in sq.m	Sr.no	Description	Area in sq.m
1	Plot	1000	1	Plot	1000
2	Set abck	100	2	Set abck	100
3	Balance plot	900	3	Balance plot	900
4	FSI from Reg 30 - Say 2.4 as per road width	2160	4	FSI from Reg 33(7) 3.00 +5%	3000
5	Set back over and above say 2 times - upto 25%	200	5	Set back over and above say 2 times	NA
6	FSI max permissible with 33(12) - 4 on net plot	upto 4.00 max on net	6	FSI max permissible with 33(12) - 1 on net plot	1
7	Balance from 33(12)	1240	7	Balance from 33(12)	900
8	Total permissible with combination	3600	8	Total permissible with combination	3900

Cluster redevelopment of cessed buildings

In the Island City, there are 14,207 cessed buildings that have the potential for redevelopment. This activity is expected to receive a boost as it has become more profitable. The redevelopment projects will provide a good source of retail supply and promote healthy housing. Most of the cessed buildings are located in Ward B, C, D, and E, with areas such as Tardeo, Grant Road, Girgaon, Bhuleshwar, Pydhoni, Bhendi Bazaar, Sandhurst Road, Chira Bazar, and Nagpada likely to undergo redevelopment. The congested Island City region can also benefit from the Cluster Development Scheme, which provides another opportunity for revamping. Ongoing projects such as the reconstruction of BDD Chawls at Worli and Naigaon and projects in Parel are already underway. Other cluster development projects may emerge as incentives are being offered for ongoing ones. Furthermore, Mumbai Port Trust (MbPT), a special planning authority, is planning to release 282.5 Ha of land from its holdings along the eastern coastal area to the city. Out of this, 187.5 Ha will be developed as public open space, 18 Ha earmarked for tourism and entertainment purposes, and 69.64 Ha for commercial development to fund the overall project.

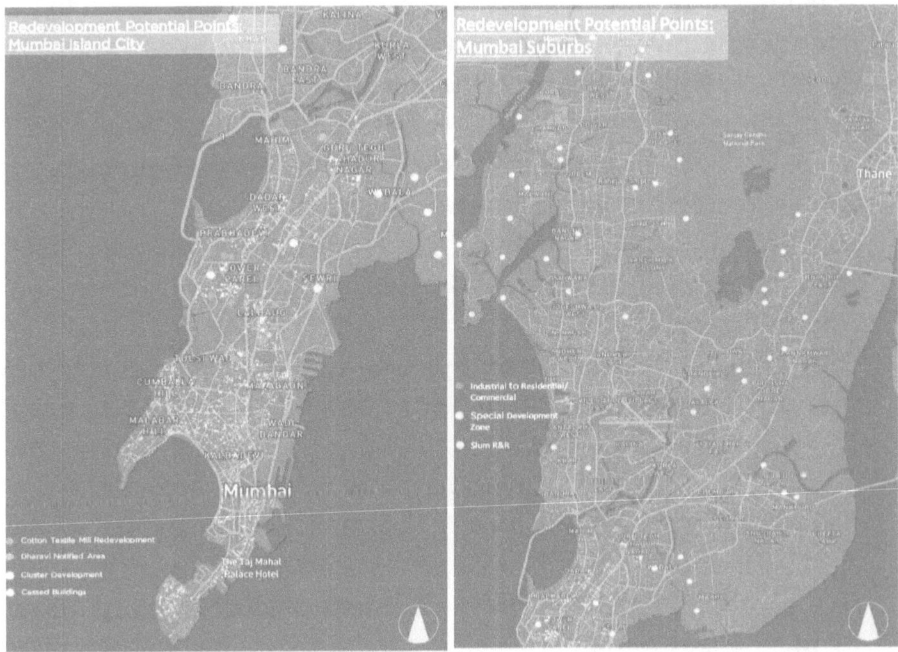

Case Studies

a. BDD Chawl- Mumbai

- The BDD Chawl reconstruction project is a significant redevelopment initiative in Mumbai that aims to enhance the quality of life for those living in one of the city's oldest and most crowded neighbourhoods. Over 16,000 people live in BDD Chawls, a collection of over 160 dilapidated structures in Mumbai's Worli, Naigaon, and NM Joshi Marg.

- In collaboration with private developers, the Maharashtra Housing and Area Development Authority (MHADA) is carrying out the reconstruction project. The project would take ten years to complete when it was started in 2017. The present chawls will be demolished as part of the rehabilitation plan, and new structures with contemporary facilities will be built.

- Elevators, fire suppression equipment, and energy-saving measures will all be included in the new structures. The project also involves building new streets, public areas, and neighbourhood amenities, including markets, hospitals, and schools. The initiative intends to improve living conditions for locals and expand housing the supply while protecting the region's cultural heritage.

- The redevelopment proposal will give inhabitants news that is equal in size to or larger than their current homes. Rehabilitating current residents residing in the Chawls for decades is also a part of the initiative. The initiative intends to improve the locals' living circumstances and quality of life while maintaining the region's cultural history.

- The project has, however, encountered several difficulties, such as delays in the permitting procedure, legal battles, and opposition from certain locals who worry about losing their houses. The project has undergone multiple adjustments to address these issues and ensure the participation and backing of all stakeholders.

- Overall, the BDD Chawl redevelopment project is a huge effort to raise the standard of living for locals in one of Mumbai's oldest and busiest districts. In order to encourage proper and environmentally-conscious urban growth, it is important to emphasise the collaboration between the government, private developers, and citizens.

b. Bhendi Bazaar, Mumbai

- The Bhendi Bazaar rebuilding Project is one of Mumbai's most famous rebuilding initiatives. This project aims to revitalise a South Mumbai neighbourhood with a rich history and a population of over 20,000 people, many of whom live in small, decaying homes. The initiative intends to modernise and sustainably develop the neighbourhood while protecting its cultural value and offering people better homes and amenities.
- The Saifee Burhani Upliftment Trust (SBUT), a nonprofit organisation connected to the Dawoodi Bohra community, is responsible for the project. The project started in 2009 and shall be finished in stages, within the following few years.
- Over 250 buildings will be demolished as part of the redevelopment plan, and approximately 17 high-rise structures will be built, adding over 3,000 additional residential and commercial units. Modern conveniences, including lifts, fire safety measures and energy-saving elements, will be included in the new structures. Along with renovating various historic structures, the project also entails the installation of new roads, parks, and public areas.
- Numerous obstacles must be overcome for the project to succeed, including the need to move thousands of people during construction and the need to protect the region's historic heritage. The SBUT has collaborated closely with locals, community leaders, and government agencies to solve these issues and ensure the project benefits all parties involved.

c. The Redevelopment of King's Cross Central, London

The redevelopment of King's Cross Central in London is a fantastic example of how an old industrial area can be transformed into a thriving and diverse neighbourhood. The project aimed to breathe new life into the once-neglected space, creating a sustainable and inclusive urban environment that people would love to live, work, and visit. The result is a vibrant mix of offices, homes, shops, and cultural spaces that have rejuvenated the neighbourhood while preserving its historical charm.

Bringing New Life to Old Buildings:

The redevelopment project honoured the area's rich history by repurposing and restoring historic buildings. Structures like the Granary Building and the Victorian gas holders were given a new lease on life, blending their unique character with modern design elements. This approach helped retain the area's identity and added a touch of charm to the revitalised neighbourhood.

A Place for Everyone:

The redevelopment project focused on creating a mixed-use community where people could live, work, and play. It introduced diverse spaces, including offices, homes, shops, restaurants, and public areas. This mix of uses has made the neighbourhood vibrant and dynamic, providing opportunities for people of all backgrounds to come together and enjoy the area.

Spaces to Enjoy:

The project put a strong emphasis on creating high-quality public spaces and amenities. Parks, squares, and green areas were introduced, giving residents and visitors places to relax, socialise, and enjoy nature. Additionally, cultural amenities such as art installations, galleries, and performance spaces were incorporated, adding a touch of creativity and making the neighbourhood an exciting hub for cultural experiences.

Better Transportation and Connectivity:

Efforts were made to improve transportation and connectivity in the area. The redevelopment project integrated King's Cross and St. Pancras International railway stations into the development, making it easier for people to access the neighbourhood. Pedestrian and cycling infrastructure was also enhanced, encouraging sustainable modes of transportation and reducing dependence on cars.

A Sustainable and Innovative Approach:

The project placed a significant emphasis on sustainability. The redevelopment incorporated energy-efficient buildings, renewable energy sources, and innovative water management systems. Features like green roofs, rainwater harvesting, and sustainable drainage systems were implemented to reduce the environmental impact and create a greener neighbourhood.

Working Together with the Community:

The project heavily relied on community engagement. The residents and stakeholders had an active role in the planning process, ensuring their opinions were valued and their needs were addressed. Working together with community groups, schools, and local organisations helped establish a neighbourhood that represents the diverse aspirations of its inhabitants.

Conclusion:

The King's Cross Central redevelopment is a remarkable example of how a neglected area can be transformed into a thriving and inclusive community. The project has breathed new life into the neighbourhood by repurposing old buildings, creating a mix of spaces, enhancing public areas, prioritising sustainability, and involving the community. The result is a vibrant, diverse, and sustainable area that people can proudly call home. The redevelopment of King's Cross Central showcases the power of thoughtful and inclusive urban planning in creating a neighbourhood that meets the aspirations and needs of its residents while preserving its historical heritage.

Redevelopment Reshaping Mumbai: The effect of Redevelopment on the City of Dreams

- The redevelopment of dilapidated buildings has significantly improved the quality of life in many areas. Modern structures with better amenities have replaced old ones, which last longer due to the use of advanced technology and careful planning. This has reduced the need for occupants to keep up with maintenance. The newly rebuilt areas have a modern and cleaner appearance, giving them a fresh identity. Hygiene and cleanliness are maintained, which is essential for a healthy living environment.
- Cluster redevelopment is becoming increasingly popular and holds a lot of promise for the future. The new structures have

resulted in more cohesive suburban planning and a consistent look throughout the area. Previously neglected areas have been transformed, offering residents access to many facilities and recreational spaces in the city, promoting a sense of community.

- Mumbai's continuous construction means that the city skyline is changing rapidly. Redevelopment will reshape the skyline of Mumbai to another level.
- The BMC is working hard to ensure an effective and efficient approval process, making the redevelopment process smoother and more accessible for all.

Chapter 11

Types of FSI

Introduction

Land development and its regulations play a crucial role in shaping urban landscapes and determining the density of cities. In India, land development falls under the jurisdiction of the states, resulting in variations in regulations across different cities. One key aspect of land development regulations is the Floor Space Index (FSI), which governs the permissible built-up area on a given plot of land. This chapter explores FSI policies in Mumbai and provides a comparative analysis of FSI policies in cities around the World.

FSI policy in Mumbai

In urban planning and development, Floor Space Index (FSI) policies play a significant role in shaping the skyline and determining the density of cities. Mumbai, the financial capital of India, has been at the centre of discussions regarding FSI regulations due to its booming population and limited land availability. We will delve into a comparative analysis of FSI policies in Mumbai and various cities across the globe, exploring their strengths, weaknesses, and impacts on urban development.

Mumbai faces several challenges, including limited land resources and a significant portion of its population living in slums. It must balance accommodating its growing population and maintaining its status as India's financial capital. To address these challenges, the development control rules in Mumbai are crucial.

The Maharashtra Regional and Town Planning Act (MRTP), 1969, mandates the development of regional plans and development plans for 20 years in regions and municipalities of Maharashtra. Currently, the state has two development plans, DCPR 2034 for Mumbai and UDCPR for the rest of the state, to simplify the regulations. DCPR 2034 is based on accommodation and Reservation policy.

DCPR 2034: Sustainable Redevelopment of Mumbai

DCPR 2034 refers to the revised Development Control and Promotion Regulations for Mumbai, which were introduced in 2018 and intended to shape the city's development and address various urban planning aspects until 2034.

Why is DCPR 2034 necessary?

To boost Mumbai's economic potential, it's important to focus on both new development and the redevelopment of private housing societies, cessed buildings, slums, and MHADA colonies. Land in Mumbai remains a scarce commodity, and thus redevelopment is crucial for the city's future. Hence, a policy framework is needed to promote redevelopment sustainably and bring about meaningful change on the ground.

The newly framed development plan (DP) emphasises sustainable development by balancing the city's economic growth, protecting the environment and ensuring social justice for its citizens. It envisions a faster pace of change for Mumbai, an improved living

environment and enhanced provisions of equitable livelihood and physical and social infrastructure.

As of September 1st, 2018, the DCPR 2034 took effect. Some of its provisions were later notified on November 13th, 2018. It will govern all the building development activity and development work in the exclusive jurisdiction of MCGM for the next two decades.

Permissible FSI = [Base + Premium FSI + TDR] + Fungible FSI.

Base FSI: Base FSI refers to the basic Floor Space Index (FSI) allowed for a plot of land. It is the starting point for calculating the total permissible FSI for a plot, which considers various factors such as road width, zone (residential/commercial), and other factors such as premium FSI and TDR (Transferable Development Rights).

Premium FSI: Premium FSI refers to an additional Floor Space Index (FSI) that a developer or landowner can purchase from the local authorities. This additional FSI is over and above the base FSI allowed for a plot of land.

The cost of purchasing premium FSI is usually determined by the local authorities and is based on factors such as the location of the plot, the prevailing market rates, and other factors.

TDR: TDR stands for Transferable Development Rights. It is a tool used by urban planners to transfer development rights from one plot of land to another. Under DCPR 2034, TDR is linked to road width and is permitted for greater road width but restricted on roads less than 9 metres wide.

TDR works on a floating FSI concept that allows landowners or developers to transfer the development rights of their plots to another plot, usually in exchange for compensation. This can be useful when a plot of land has development restrictions, such as being located in a heritage zone or having environmental constraints. DCPR dictates that 50 – 60% of TDR should come from non-Slum TDR.

Types of TDR: In Mumbai, different types of Transferable Development Rights (TDR) can be used as incentives by the government. These include:

- **Reservation TDR:** This type of TDR is generated when a builder gives up land that is reserved for other purposes in the Development Plan. E.g. Road widening TDR.
- **Slum TDR:** This type of TDR is generated when a developer takes up a slum redevelopment project.
- **Heritage TDR:** This type of TDR allows owners of heritage buildings to transfer their development rights to another plot in exchange for the conservation and restoration of their heritage building.

Fungible FSI: Fungible FSI allows builders to construct additional floors beyond the fixed FSI limit by paying a premium calculated based on the Ready Reckoner Rates of the area. It was introduced in the new DCPR for compensating the inclusion of "Free of FSI" space such as balcony, flower beds, terraces, voids, niches, etc.

In residential properties in Mumbai, the norm specifies that the Fungible FSI should not exceed 35 per cent of the floor area. At the same time, in industrial and commercial developments, the permissible limit is 20 percent of the floor area.

Example: Let's say we have a plot of land in the island city of Mumbai that is located on a road that is 10 metres wide. According to DCPR 2034, for a road that is between 9.0 metres and 12.0 metres wide in the island city, the permissible FSI is calculated as follows: 1.33 (Basic) + 0.5 (Premium FSI) + 0.17 (TDR) = 2.00 (Permissible FSI) + up to 35% Fungible over and above.

This means that for our plot of land on a 10-metre-wide road in the island city, the permissible FSI would be 2.00 + up to 35% Fungible over and above.

The Permissible FSI limits are also governed by the schemes under which the development of a project takes place.

Is DCPR 2034 better than its Predecessor?

To differentiate between DCR 1991 and DCPR 2034, some quantitative analysis is beneficial to put things in context.

The recent DCPR 2034 has maintained the base FSI, but introduced Premium FSI and TDR to grant additional FSI. This has led to considerable progress in the Island City. Meanwhile, suburban areas have experienced no change in FSI, except for plots that face narrow roads of less than 9m. This emphasises the importance of wider roads or road widening to match the construction scale. Although the overall development potential in suburbs has slightly increased, it is calculated based on the gross plot area, which includes RG (Recreation Ground) and reservation area for loading Premium FSI and TDR.

FOR ISLAND CITY (RESIDENTIAL)

		Prior to DCPR 2034				
Road width	Basic	Additional FSI on payment of Premium	Admissible TDR	Permissible FSI	Add Fungible FSI @	Total FSI
Column	A	B	C	D = A + B + C	E	F = D * (1+E)
up to 9m	1.33	-	-	1.33	35%	1.80
9m - 12m	1.33	-	0.17	1.50	35%	2.03
12 m - 18m	1.33	-	0.37	1.70	35%	2.30
18 m - 27m	1.33	-	0.57	1.90	35%	2.57
>27 m	1.33	-	0.87	2.00	35%	2.70

As per DCPR 2034						Difference
Basic	Additional FSI on payment of Premium	Admissible TDR	Permissible FSI	Add Fungible FSI @	Total FSI	
G	H	I	J = G + H + I	K	L = J*(1+K)	M = L - F
1.33	0.00	0.00	1.33	35%	1.80	0.00
1.33	0.50	0.17	2.00	35%	2.70	0.68
1.33	0.62	0.45	2.40	35%	3.24	0.95
1.33	0.73	0.64	2.70	35%	3.65	1.08
1.33	0.84	0.83	3.00	35%	4.05	1.35

Source: Knight Frank Research, DCPR 2034

FOR SUBURBS (RESIDENTIAL)

		Prior to DCPR 2034				
Road width	Basic	Additional FSI on payment of Premium	Admissible TDR	Permissible FSI	Add Fungible FSI @	Total FSI
Column	A	B	C	D = A + B + C	E	F = D * (1+E)
up to 9m	1.0	0.5	-	1.50	35%	2.03
9m - 12m	1.0	0.5	0.5	2.00	35%	2.70
12 m - 18m	1.0	0.5	0.7	2.20	35%	2.97
18 m - 27m	1.0	0.5	0.9	2.40	35%	3.24
>27 m	1.0	0.5	1.0	2.50	35%	3.375

As per DCPR 2034						Difference
Basic	Additional FSI on payment of Premium	Admissible TDR	Permissible FSI	Add Fungible FSI @	Total FSI	
G	H	I	J = G + H + I	K	L = J*(1+K)	M = L - F
1.0	0.0	0.0	1.00	35%	1.35	-0.675
1.0	0.5	0.5	2.00	35%	2.70	No difference
1.0	0.5	0.7	2.20	35%	2.97	No difference
1.0	0.5	0.9	2.40	35%	3.24	No difference
1.0	0.5	1.0	2.50	35%	3.375	No difference

Source: Knight Frank Research, DCPR 2034

Slum rehabilitation

Over the last two decades, only 100,000 slum units have been rehabilitated in Mumbai under the current slum rehabilitation policy. At this rate, it would take around 300 years to rehabilitate the 15-16 lakh slum units in the city. The current DCPR 2034 may perpetuate the shortcomings of the previous policy by retaining the same standards.

Slum-free Mumbai and Affordable housing for all

Around 41% of Mumbai's population resides in slums or slum-like conditions. Shortage of affordable housing is persistent in Mumbai, and the demand-supply gap is consistently growing despite several policy interventions by both central and state governments. Specifically, the housing gap for the Economically Weaker Section (EWS) and Low Income Group (LIG) population is enormous, creating slum clusters in prime areas within Mumbai. DCPR is vital to accommodate future housing needs and offer a better dwelling experience to the slum and its residents. Hence the city needs to create adequate, affordable housing stock.

Clubbing of Schemes

The Slum Rehabilitation Authority (SRA) is a government body established to be a planning authority for all slum areas in the Municipal Corporation of Greater Mumbai jurisdiction. The Government of Maharashtra has introduced a scheme to rehabilitate slums by allowing the use of land as a resource. Incentives in the form of floor space index (FSI) are provided for tenements that can be sold in the open market. This is done for cross-subsidisation of the slum rehabilitation tenements, which will be provided free to the slum-dwellers.

Clubbing of schemes refers to the process of combining multiple SRA schemes under the Development Control and Promotion Regulation (DCPR) 2034. This can be done for schemes on slum plots, non-slum plots or a combination of both. Clubbing of schemes is usually done to maximise the potential of development over a plot.

TDR

Transferable Development Rights (TDR) is compensation in the form of Floor Space Index (FSI) or Development Rights which shall entitle the owner for construction of built-up area subject to provisions in this regulation. This FSI credit shall be issued in a certificate which shall be called as Development Right Certificate (DRC).

Development Rights Certificate {DRC} shall be issued by Municipal Commissioner under his signature and endorse thereon in writing in figures and in words, the FSI credit in square meters of the built-up area to which the owner or lessee is entitled, the place from where it is generated and the rate of that plot as prescribed in the Annual Statement of Rates issued by the Registration Department for the concerned year.

Cases eligible for TDR:

- Lands under various reservations for public purposes, new roads, road widening etc. which are subjected to acquisition, proposed in Draft or Final Development Plan, prepared under the provisions of the Maharashtra Regional and Town Planning Act, 1966
- Lands under any deemed reservations according to any regulations prepared as per the provisions of Maharashtra Regional & Town Planning Act, 1966
- Lands under any new road or road widening proposed under the provisions of Mumbai Municipal Corporation Act, 1888
- Development or construction of the amenity on the reserved land
- unutilized FST of any structure or precinct which is declared as Heritage structure or Precinct under the provisions of Development Control Regulations, due to restrictions imposed in that regulation;
- In lieu of constructing housing for slum-dwellers according to regulations prepared under the Maharashtra Regional & Town Planning Act, 1966
- The purposes as may be notified by the Government from time to time, by way of, modification to, new addition of, any of the provisions of sanctioned Development Control Regulations

Cases not eligible for TDR:

- For earlier land acquisition or development for which compensation has been already paid partly or fully by any means
- Where award of land has already been declared and which is valid under the Land Acquisition Act, 1894 or the Right to Fair Compensation & Transparency in Land Acquisition, Rehabilitation and Resettlement Act, 2013 unless lands are withdrawn from the award by the Appropriate Authority according to the provisions of the relevant Acts
- In cases where layout has already been sanctioned and layout roads are incorporated as Development Plan roads prior to these regulations.
- In cases where layout is submitted along with proposed Development Plan Road, in such cases. TDR shall not be permissible for the width of road that would be necessary according to the length as per Development Control Regulations
- If the compensation in the form of FSI / or by any means has already been granted to the owner
- Where lawful possession including by mutual agreement /or contract has been taken.
- For an existing user or retention user or any required compulsory open space or recreational open space or recreational ground, in any layout.
- For any designation, allocation of the use or zone which is not subjected to acquisition.

TDR generation

- TDR against surrender of Land
- TDR against construction of amenities

Utilisation of TDR:

Sr. No.	Plots fronting on road width (in Meter)	Maximum Permissible TDR Loading in Greater Mumbai	
		TDR in Island City	TDR in Suburb/ Extended Suburb
1	2	3	4
1.	less than 9.00 m	---	---
2.	9 m. and above but less than 12.20m	0.17	0.50
3.	12.20 m. and above but less than 18.30 m.	0.37	0.70
4.	18.30 m. and above but less than 30.00 m.	0.57	0.90
5.	30 m. and above	0.67	1.00

FSI across different Indian States

STATE/ CITIES	MULTISTOREY BUILDINGS	SPECIAL BUIDINGS
Ahmedabad, Gujarat	1.2 upto 5.4	
Patna, Bihar	2-2.5 & max 2.5	
Bengaluru, Karnataka	1.75 & 3.25	
Bhopal, MP	1.25 & 2.50	1.5 to 2.25 (public and semi-public offerings
Chennai, TN	3.25	2
Delhi	2 to 3.5	
Gandhinagar, Gujarat	R1 & R2- 1.8 upto 4 and R3-0.3	2
Gurugram, Haryana	2.40 to 2.64	4
Hyderabad, Telangana	NO FSI	
Jaipur, Rajasthan	Built up Area Ratio (BAR) are permissible 2.00	
Ranchi, Jharkhand	1.5 to 3	3 to 3.5

STATE/ CITIES	MULTISTOREY BUILDINGS	SPECIAL BUIDINGS
Kerala	3 to 4	4
Kolkata, WB	1.75 to 3.6	
Lucknow, UP	1.25 to 1.50	
Mumbai, Maharashtra	Mumbai Island City : 2.4 Mumbai Suburbs : 2.2	
Noida, UP	2.75 to 3.5	5.32
Pune, Maharashtra	1.1. to 1.3*- In case of TOD 1.1 to 1.4* In addition to the above 60% /80% ancillary FSI Permitted. * Based upon Road Width size of the plot	Same as Cl no 2

Shelter Fee Across States:

STATE	SHELTER
Andhra Pradesh	Land extent more than 3000 Sq.mtrs and upto 5 acres (including 5 acres), (2.023 Hectares) shall provide 10% of the total built up area towards the EWS / LIG units.
Gujarat	10% of the total built up area towards the EWS / LIG units.
Haryana	The area of a project is above five acres, builder or developer should provide 10% of the total built-up area to EWS and LIG (5% each) or 25% of the total number of housing units to the two sections (12.5 % each).
Jharkhand	Provision of providing 10% of total built up area or 20% of total number of units towards EWS & LIG within the site or within 5kms of site.
Karnataka	Reservation mandated in projects of Private Developers: housing stock, reservation will be mandated for, in order to increase affordable housing in all projects of area 1 hectare or more.
Kerala	No public funds collection towards shelter fund in Kerala. For affordable houses to EWS, the State Government directly heads it from state spending and from PMAY scheme based on its accessibility.

STATE	SHELTER
Madhya Pradesh	The area of plots and constructed area of the constructed residential units reserved for economically weaker sections and low-income group shall be as follow:- For economically weaker section : Develop plots - 30 to 40 sq mtr Residential units - 25 to 35 sq mtr For low-income group : Develop plots - 41 to 96 sq mtr .Residential units - 36 to 48 sq mtr
Maharashtra	For the plot of land admeasuring 4000 Sq. Mtrs. or more (after deducting R.P/ D.P road reservations etc.), EWS/LIG housing in the form of tenements of size ranging between 30-50 Sq. Mtrs. carpet area shall be constructed at least to the extent of 20% of the basic (1.1) FSI which shall be over and above the permissible FSI. To be handed over to MHADA, at the construction cost mentioned in the ASR for the year of disposal + 25% additional cost. (Refer Chapter 3 Clause 3.8 sub clause (b) of UDCPR 2020) For PMAY which is monitored by MHADA, stamp duty is Rs.1000/- and registration 1%. The GST charged to the homebuyers under PMAY is 1% Under PMAY, the GST charged by the developer to the contractor is 12 % with no input credit, where the normal charges are 18%.
Rajasthan	For Residential Buildings Rs. 10/- per sq mtr on Gross Built up area and for commercial Buildings Rs. 25/- per sq mtr on Gross Built up area.

STATE	SHELTER
Tamil Nadu	Shelter fund being collected as per G.O. Ms. No. 31, Housing and Urban Development Department dated 31.01.2020. After deducting 3000 sq.m as follows :- 1. Commercial and IT Building - 1.2% of GLV 2. Residential and Industrial - 1.1% of GLV 3. Institutional building - 1.0% of GLV
Telangana	Rs 600 per Sq Mtr
Uttrakhand	15% of the total Housing stock proposed in the project for EWS Housing
Uttar Pradesh	No collection of shelter fund. It is undertaken from State allocation fund for affordable housing.

Comparison of FSI policies in cities around the World

Comparing FSI policies across cities worldwide is crucial for understanding them completely. Here are some examples of FSI policies in different cities:

Tokyo, Japan:

Tokyo's FSI policy stands out for its unique approach to urban development. The city has embraced a high FSI, allowing for tall buildings and efficient land utilisation. This has resulted in a compact urban landscape, maximising land use efficiency and promoting efficient public transport systems. However, the policy necessitates careful planning to balance high density and preserving open spaces. Tokyo's FSI policy allows for high-rise buildings and efficient land utilisation. FSI limits can range from **6.0 to 15.0**, with some districts permitting even higher limits. This approach results in a compact urban environment, maximising land efficiency.

New York City, USA:

New York City's FSI policy reflects a mixed approach, with variations across different zones. The city has areas with high-density zoning, such as Manhattan, where skyscrapers dominate the skyline. In contrast, other areas have lower FSI limits to preserve historic sites or maintain a neighbourhood's character. This approach aims to balance growth and preservation, catering to the city's diverse needs. Depending on the zoning district, FSI limits in New York City can range from **5.0 to 15.0**. The high limits accommodate the city's growing population and demand for commercial and residential spaces.

Singapore:

Singapore has a highly regulated FSI policy that focuses on meticulous urban planning. The city-state's comprehensive approach ensures sustainable growth and efficient land use. FSI limits are set based on infrastructure capacity, environmental considerations, and public amenities. By adopting a holistic approach, Singapore has created a well-designed urban landscape with green spaces, efficient transportation networks, and quality living environments. FSI limits in Singapore vary based on different zones. The limits range from **2.8 to 25.0**, with higher limits in areas designated for high-density development, such as the Central Business District.

São Paulo, Brazil:

São Paulo has faced challenges similar to Mumbai regarding rapid urbanisation and population growth. The city's FSI policy has evolved to address these issues, emphasising mixed-use developments and promoting densification in specific areas. However, the policy implementation has faced challenges, including inadequate infrastructure and the emergence of informal settlements. São Paulo's experience highlights the importance of comprehensive planning and infrastructure development alongside FSI policies. FSI limits in São Paulo vary across different zones. They range from **1.0 to 4.0**, allowing for varying density levels in different parts of the city.

Chapter 12

Hyderabad: The Land of Unlimited FSI

Introduction

Telangana became a separate state on June 2, 2014, after separating from Andhra Pradesh. Initially, Hyderabad was declared the joint capital of both states for ten years until 2024. However, in 2019, Andhra Pradesh announced Amravati as its capital. Hyderabad continues to have the highest share in demand and supply of real estate units across all asset classes and all south Indian cities. Additionally, significant changes have yet to be made to building bylaws since forming the new state.

In 2006, a decision was made to allow unlimited FSI to attract investment. However, building height was still subject to regulations such as plot layout, access, road width, setback requirements, and reservations from authorities. This policy enabled builders to maximise the potential of plots on the city outskirts. However, the same was different for the city centre, which had developed haphazardly with numerous unauthorised constructions, making it difficult for plots to overcome regulations and obtain higher height limits. To address poor planning, the city launched the GHMC LRS (Layout Regularization Scheme) to reorganise the city. While builders in the outskirts took advantage of larger plots with better access and fewer restrictions to construct taller and denser complexes, the policy needed to produce the expected changes in the urban core part of the city.

Development Control Rules

Hyderabad has two primary authorities responsible for granting building permission and clearances based on jurisdiction - the Greater Hyderabad Municipal Council (GHMC) and the Hyderabad Urban Development Authority (HUDA). Following the Telangana Municipalities Act 2019, the Telangana government has introduced TS-bPASS (Telangana State Building Permission Approval and Self Certification System). This single integrated platform enables the processing of various permissions required for land development and building construction through a self-certification system. This new system has made obtaining permission and monitoring applications' status much simpler.

For small plot sizes, there is no permission required up to a certain height. Buildings higher than 18 metres are characterised as High rises in Hyderabad and should have a minimum plot size of 2000 sqm. These can be both Residential or Commercial projects based on land use. For High Rise Building/Complex, the minimum required road width and open space/setback on all sides should meet the following standards:-

Height of building (in metres)		Minimum road width required (in metres)	Minimum all-round open space on remaining sides (in metres)
Above	Up to		
1	2	3	4
-	21	12	7
21	24	12	8
24	27	18	9
27	30	18	10
30	35	24	11
35	40	24	12
40	45	24	13
45	40	30	14
50	44	30	16
After 55m, 0.5m additional setback for every 5m height shall be insisted.			

(Andhra Pradesh Building Rules, 2012)

The Unlimited Floor Space Index (FSI) policy applies to residential and commercial projects. If the construction project meets the designated land use, setback requirements, height limits, and complies with the National Building Code (NBC), and obtains the necessary No Objection Certificates (NOC) from the competent authorities, there are no restrictions on FSI, and the construction plan is likely to receive approval from the competent authority. However, it is essential to acknowledge that additional requirements may exist based on the specific regulations and policies of the jurisdiction in question.

Pros and Cons of Unlimited FSI Policy in Hyderabad

Pros	Explanation
Increased development potential	Unlimited FSI allows for higher building densities and increased development potential, leading to more housing and commercial spaces in the city. This can help address Hyderabad's growing population and demand for real estate.
Optimal land utilisation	With unlimited FSI, developers can better use available land by constructing taller buildings, reducing the need for sprawling developments. It promotes vertical growth, which can be beneficial in land-scarce areas.
Economic growth and investment opportunities	The policy can attract more investments and promote economic growth in the construction and real estate sectors. It can create job opportunities and contribute to the overall development of the city's infrastructure.
Affordable housing possibilities	Higher FSI can lead to more affordable housing options as it increases the supply of housing units in the market, which helps address the issue of housing affordability for certain segments of the population.

Cons	Explanation
The strain on existing infrastructure	Unlimited FSI can put significant strain on the existing infrastructure, including roads, utilities, and public services. The sudden increase in population density may lead to congestion, inadequate services, and increased pressure on resources.
Potential for overdevelopment	Unlimited FSI can lead to overdevelopment and a mismatch between infrastructure capacity and population density without proper regulations and oversight. This can result in a poorly planned urban environment and compromised livability.
Impact on Heritage and Aesthetics	Unlimited FSI may lead to tall buildings that could overshadow and detract from the city's heritage structures, architectural character, and visual appeal. It could impact the cultural and historical identity of Hyderabad.
Environmental concerns	High-density development resulting from unlimited FSI can have adverse environmental consequences, such as increased energy consumption, water demand, and waste generation. It may also contribute to the loss of green spaces and negatively affect the urban ecosystem.

It's important to note that the pros and cons mentioned here are general considerations and may vary based on specific contexts, regulations, and implementation of the FSI policy in Hyderabad.

Impact of Unlimited FSI in Hyderabad

The unlimited FSI policy has enabled the construction of the tallest building in the city, Lodha Bellezza, which stands at 153 metres. However, soon it will be surpassed by SAS Crown, which will be 228 metres tall. Residential and commercial projects in Gachibowli, Manikonda, Madhapur, Narsingi, Hi-Tech City, and Kokapet have average FSI limits of 6-7 and even surpass 10 in some cases. Recently, there have been concerns that some builders are exploiting the unlimited FSI policy, as evidenced by the presence of high-rise, dense complexes next to large open spaces that result in patchy development. In an April 2022 meeting, KT Rama Rao requested that builders in the city consider water availability, parking facilities, waste management, and sewage management during construction and planning. The government will continue with the unlimited FSI plan for their benefit, but if they fail to plan properly with basic amenities in mind, the government will impose strict rules.

Lodha Bellezza: Lodha Bellezza is known for its premium amenities and high-end apartments. The project offers spacious and well-designed residences with modern features and finishes. It is spread across approximately 10 acres of land and has several high-rise towers.

The apartments in Lodha Bellezza are available in various configurations, including 3 BHK, 4 BHK, and penthouses. The project boasts lavish interiors, panoramic views, and amenities like swimming pools, landscaped gardens, a clubhouse, a gymnasium, sports facilities, and 24/7 security.

Lodha Bellezza is situated in the posh area of Kukatpally, providing easy access to different parts of Hyderabad. Its proximity to significant IT centres, educational institutions, healthcare facilities, shopping malls, and recreational areas make it a desirable option for residents.

SAS Crown: SAS Crown is the new High-rise uber-luxury residential project launched in Kokapet, Outer Ring Road, Hyderabad.

Crown is an ultra-luxury residential enclave that proudly claims to be the tallest residential skyscraper in South India. Created by SAS Infra, this lavish living space offers king-sized apartments with spacious layouts and extravagant features.

SAS Crown offers its guests a wide range of amenities, including a fully equipped clubhouse spanning 100,000 square feet. There are guest suites, a restaurant with a chef on-call, a gym, an Olympic-sized swimming pool with a sun deck and jacuzzi, recreation rooms, spa and yoga areas, multiple sports courts, a party hall, a conference hall and more. These amenities have been meticulously planned with the utmost importance placed on state-of-the-art 24/7 security measures.

(Fig: SAS Crown)

Summary:

Therefore, FSI norms in Hyderabad significantly impact the city's development and environment. While unlimited FSI can offer some advantages for developers and residents, it can also create problems for the city's planning and management. Hence, there is a need for a balanced approach that considers both the benefits and drawbacks of FSI norms in Hyderabad.

Chapter 13

How to Make Mumbai Great Again!

Overview of Mumbai and MMR

Mumbai, often called the "City of Dreams," has faced numerous challenges recently, including overcrowding, inadequate infrastructure, and urban decay. Revitalising the city while adhering to development control norms is essential to create a sustainable, vibrant, and liveable urban environment. This chapter explores strategies to revitalise Mumbai while considering the constraints and opportunities presented by development control norms.

In Mumbai, around seven million people live in slums, around 2.5 million live in cessed buildings, and around 1.2-1.5 million live in MHADA colonies. The aim of the 1991 DP policies was to enhance the quality of life and housing conditions of certain individuals. Unfortunately, these intended beneficiaries have not experienced any significant improvement as a result of these policies.

The new DCPR 2034 aims to address these challenges by opening up more land for real estate construction and promoting organised development. By enforcing these regulations and ensuring that new developments adhere to them, Mumbai can ensure sustainable development and address its real estate problems. **The Mumbai Metropolitan Region (MMR)** is a vibrant and rapidly growing region surrounding the city of Mumbai. It encompasses several urban centres, satellite towns, and rural areas.

Revitalising Mumbai is essential for improving the quality of life of residents and plays a significant role in India's overall development. Mumbai's economic prowess and status as a financial hub make its revitalisation crucial for attracting investments, boosting job creation, and promoting economic diversification. Additionally, as Mumbai is a major port city, its development is instrumental in facilitating international trade and commerce.

By addressing these challenges head-on and implementing effective development strategies, Mumbai has the potential to become a vibrant, sustainable, and inclusive city that offers its residents a high quality of life while also contributing to India's growth story.

Historical Background of Slums in Mumbai

During the late 1800s, Mumbai experienced the impact of the industrial revolution, resulting in an inhospitable living environment lacking basic civic services such as water and drainage. This area was labelled a "slum," following a similar pattern in industrial centres like Liverpool and Manchester in England. However, it was only after the bubonic plague outbreak in 1896 in Bombay that the colonial authorities were compelled to address housing and sanitation issues. In response to the plague, the Bombay Improvement Trust (BIT) was established in 1898, followed by the Bombay Development Department (BDD) creation in 1920. These organisations aimed to construct affordable housing for the numerous workers employed in mills, ports, and railway construction. Unfortunately, it is now evident that their interventions came too late and resulted in a lingering housing crisis.

After gaining independence, our approach to addressing slums and urban development mirrored that of the colonial rulers. The government's official stance was on clearing slums, as evident from the title of the central law called the Slum Clearance Act of 1956. This approach mainly aimed at denying the existence of slums and implementing schemes for their clearance. However, in the early 1970s, there was a slight shift towards a more compassionate and logical approach to improving and upgrading slums. Maharashtra was among the first states to introduce state-specific legislation known as the Maharashtra Slum Areas (Improvement and Clearance) Act of 1971. This act provided an alternative policy to slum clearance and demolition, emphasising slum improvement programs. Furthermore, efforts were made to conduct comprehensive slum censuses, with initiatives launched to issue photo passes to slum dwellers, officially recognising their presence.

The role of authorities in managing and planning for the MMR

Mumbai Metropolitan Region Development Authority (MMRDA): MMRDA is a special planning authority that covers the entire Mumbai Metropolitan Region. It was established in 1975 and is responsible for the integrated planning and development of infrastructure projects in the MMR. MMRDA oversees the development of transport systems, metro rail projects, roads, bridges, and other regional infrastructure initiatives.

Slum Rehabilitation Authority (SRA): The Slum Rehabilitation Authority was established to rehabilitate slum dwellers and improve the living conditions of slum areas in Mumbai. SRA is responsible for implementing slum redevelopment schemes and providing better housing and amenities to slum residents.

Maharashtra Housing and Area Development Authority (MHADA): MHADA is a state government authority responsible for providing affordable housing to the people of Maharashtra. It develops housing schemes, allocates houses through lotteries, and undertakes the construction of affordable housing projects in Mumbai and other parts of the state.

Mumbai Port Trust (MbPT): Mumbai Port Trust is a statutory body that manages and governs the Mumbai Port, one of the largest ports in India. While its primary focus is on port-related activities, MbPT also plays a role in developing and maintaining port areas, waterfronts, and adjoining regions.

City and Industrial Development Corporation (CIDCO): CIDCO is one of the prominent development authorities in the MMR. It was formed in 1970 and is responsible for the planned development of Navi Mumbai, a satellite city across the harbour from Mumbai. CIDCO undertakes infrastructure development, land allocation, and urban planning activities.

These are some of the major development authorities in the Mumbai Metropolitan Region. Each authority has specific jurisdiction and responsibilities regarding urban planning, infrastructure development, and housing projects within their respective areas of operation.

Challenges faced by Mumbai in terms of development

The city of Mumbai is a bustling metropolis that faces numerous development challenges. Understanding these challenges is crucial for formulating effective strategies to revitalise the city and ensure sustainable growth.

Overview of Mumbai's current state and challenges:

Rapid population growth: Mumbai's population has steadily increased, putting immense pressure on infrastructure, housing, and basic amenities. The city's current infrastructure needs to be improved to accommodate its ever-growing population.

Inadequate transportation networks: Mumbai's transportation system faces significant challenges in congestion, inefficient public transportation, and insufficient road infrastructure. Traffic congestion not only affects the daily lives of residents but also hampers the city's economic productivity.

Housing shortage: Mumbai is grappling with a severe shortage of affordable housing. The rising population, limited land availability, and increasing property prices have contributed to a housing crisis. This shortage has resulted in the proliferation of slums and informal settlements.

Environmental degradation: Mumbai is plagued by environmental issues such as air pollution, water pollution, and waste management challenges. The city's rapid urbanisation has led to the depletion of green spaces, increased pollution levels, and inadequate waste management infrastructure.

Ageing infrastructure: Much of Mumbai's existing infrastructure, including roads, bridges, and public facilities, is ageing and needs renovation and modernisation. Outdated infrastructure contributes to inefficiencies, safety concerns, and hindrances in overall development.

Current efforts being made to address the city's challenges

Let's delve into the development of the Mumbai Metropolitan Region, highlighting its significance, challenges, and key initiatives undertaken to foster sustainable growth and improve the quality of life for its residents.

Development Initiative	Description
Mumbai Metro	The Mumbai Metro is a quick transportation system designed to enhance commutes within the city. It consists of several lines linking various areas of Mumbai, offering more efficient and faster public transportation.
Coastal Road Project	The Coastal Road Project is an ambitious initiative to construct a coastal freeway along Mumbai's western coastline. The aim of the project is to ease traffic congestion and enhance connectivity between south and north Mumbai while providing scenic views of the Arabian Sea.

Development Initiative	Description
Mumbai Trans-Harbour Link	The Mumbai Trans-Harbour Link is a planned 21.8 km long bridge connecting Mumbai with Navi Mumbai. It will provide a crucial transportation link, easing traffic congestion and reducing travel time between the two areas.
Slum Rehabilitation Schemes	The government, in collaboration with organisations like the Slum Rehabilitation Authority (SRA), has implemented various slum rehabilitation schemes. These initiatives aim to upgrade the current living conditions of slum dwellers by providing them with better housing and basic amenities.
Mumbai Coastal Road Resilience Project	The Mumbai Coastal Road Resilience Project focuses on adaptation to coastal protection and climate change. It involves constructing sea walls, revetments, and other infrastructure to safeguard Mumbai's vulnerable coastline from erosion, sea-level rise, and extreme weather events.
Mumbai Port Trust Redevelopment	The Mumbai Port Trust is undertaking redevelopment initiatives to transform the port area into a vibrant mixed-use space. This includes developing commercial complexes, recreational facilities, and public spaces while preserving the historical character of the port.
Smart City Mission	Mumbai has been selected as part of the Indian government's Smart City Mission. This initiative aims to leverage technology and innovation to improve infrastructure, enhance urban services, promote sustainable development, and improve the quality of life for residents.

Development Initiative	Description
Housing for All	The government and agencies like the Maharashtra Housing and Area Development Authority (MHADA) have launched the Housing for All initiative. It focuses on providing affordable housing to low-income groups through various schemes, including subsidised housing and housing lotteries.
Navi Mumbai International Airport	The Navi Mumbai International Airport is a major infrastructure project in the MMR. It aims to alleviate congestion at Mumbai's existing airport and provide enhanced air connectivity to the region. The airport is expected to cater to the growing air travel demands of the MMR and boost economic development.
Mumbai-Ahmedabad High-Speed Rail Corridor	The Mumbai-Ahmedabad High-Speed Rail Corridor, also known as the Bullet Train project, is a significant infrastructure undertaking. It involves the construction of a high-speed railway line connecting Mumbai with Ahmedabad, reducing travel time between the two cities to a fraction of the current duration. This project aims to enhance connectivity, facilitate economic growth, and promote sustainable regional transportation.
Virar-Alibaug Multimodal Corridor	The Virar-Alibaug Multimodal Corridor is a proposed transportation corridor connecting Virar north of Mumbai to Alibaug south. This project aims to improve regional connectivity by integrating various modes of transportation, including road, rail, and waterways, thereby reducing travel time and congestion in the MMR.
Repurposing Industrial Areas	Mumbai has several industrial areas that need to be updated. The city can breathe new life into these areas while promoting economic diversification by allowing the adaptive reuse of these spaces for mixed-use developments, such as creative hubs, cultural centres, or tech parks.

Development Initiative	Description
Affordable Housing Projects	Several affordable housing projects have been launched in the MMR to address the housing needs of different income classes. These initiatives, undertaken by organisations like CIDCO and MHADA, aim to provide affordable housing options through various schemes, including subsidised housing, slum rehabilitation, and housing lotteries.
MMRDA Infrastructure Projects	The Mumbai Metropolitan Region Development Authority (MMRDA) has been spearheading various infrastructure projects in the MMR. These include the development of metro rail lines, road networks, bridges, and flyovers, aiming to improve transportation, reduce congestion, and enhance connectivity within the region.
Urban Renewal and Redevelopment	The MMR is witnessing urban renewal and redevelopment projects to revitalise older areas and transform them into modern, sustainable urban spaces. Initiatives like cluster redevelopment, heritage conservation, and urban regeneration aim to improve the quality of life, preserve architectural heritage, and enhance the urban environment in the MMR.

These initiatives showcase the ongoing development efforts in the Mumbai Metropolitan Region to address transportation challenges, promote affordable housing, improve connectivity, and revitalise urban areas. They reflect the commitment of various authorities and organisations towards sustainable development in the MMR.

Examples of successful solutions from other cities

Development Challenge	Example Solution from Another City
Traffic Congestion	Implementing a comprehensive public transportation system similar to the Metro in Delhi, India, or the MRT in Singapore. This would help reduce reliance on private vehicles and ease traffic congestion.
Affordable Housing	Adopting a mixed-income housing model like the Vancouver Affordable Housing Agency in Canada. This approach combines market-rate and subsidised housing to ensure various affordable options for different income groups.
Slum Rehabilitation	Implementing a successful slum redevelopment program like the Favela-Bairro project in Rio de Janeiro, Brazil. This initiative involved upgrading infrastructure, providing basic amenities, and improving the living conditions of slum dwellers.
Water Management	Adopting sustainable water management practices similar to the Water Sensitive Urban Design approach in Melbourne, Australia. This includes rainwater harvesting, water recycling, and efficient water use strategies to address water scarcity issues.
Coastal Protection	Implementing innovative coastal protection measures like the Delta Works in the Netherlands. This could involve constructing storm surge barriers, dikes, and flood protection infrastructure to mitigate the impact of rising sea levels and cyclones.
Heritage Conservation	Establishing a comprehensive heritage conservation program akin to the Historic Districts Council in New York City, USA. This initiative would identify and protect historical buildings, promote adaptive reuse, and preserve Mumbai's architectural heritage.

Development Challenge	Example Solution from Another City
Waste Management	Implementing an efficient waste management system inspired by the waste-to-energy model in Stockholm, Sweden. This includes waste segregation, recycling, composting, and generating energy from waste to reduce landfill dependency and promote a circular economy.
Urban Green Spaces	Creating and maintaining urban green spaces similar to Singapore's Gardens by the Bay. This involves developing parks, gardens, and green rooftops to enhance the city's aesthetics, improve air quality, and provide recreational areas for residents.
Waste Reduction	Implementing a citywide zero-waste initiative like San Francisco's Zero Waste Program in the United States. This involves promoting recycling, composting, and reducing waste generation through education, incentives, and strict regulations.
Smart City Technology	Adopting smart city technologies similar to the Songdo International Business District in Incheon, South Korea. This includes the integration of digital infrastructure, smart grids, intelligent transportation systems, and data-driven urban management for enhanced efficiency and sustainability.
Vertical Urbanisation	Embracing vertical urbanisation strategies like the Sky City project in Changsha, China. This involves constructing tall, mixed-use buildings with residential, commercial, and recreational spaces within a compact footprint, allowing for efficient land utilisation and reducing urban sprawl.

Development Challenge	Example Solution from Another City
Urban Farming	Implementing urban farming initiatives like the Incredible Edible project in Todmorden, UK. This involves converting underutilised spaces into community gardens, rooftop farms, and vertical farms to promote local food production, improve food security, and enhance community engagement.
Digital Inclusion	Establishing digital inclusion programs like the Digital Equity Initiative in Barcelona, Spain. This initiative focuses on providing access to digital technologies, digital literacy training, and bridging the digital divide to ensure equitable access to information and opportunities for all residents.
Climate Resilience	Developing climate-resilient infrastructure inspired by the Resilient by Design program in the San Francisco Bay Area, USA. This involves incorporating resilient design principles, such as green infrastructure, flood-resistant buildings, and coastal protection measures, to withstand climate change impacts like flooding and extreme weather events.
Public Space Activation	Activating underutilised public spaces like the High Line in New York City, USA. This involves transforming abandoned railway tracks or unused areas into vibrant public parks, pedestrian walkways, and cultural hubs to enhance livability and community interaction.
Energy Efficiency	Implementing energy-efficient building standards like the Passive House concept in Germany. This includes designing and constructing energy-efficient buildings with high insulation, airtightness, and renewable energy systems to reduce energy consumption and carbon emissions.

Suggestions for Revitalising MMR

Revitalisation Suggestions	Description
Urban Greening	Promote urban greening initiatives by creating more parks, gardens, and green spaces throughout the MMR. This will enhance the quality of life, improve air quality, and provide recreational areas for residents.
Mixed-Use Development	Encourage mixed-use development that combines residential, commercial, and recreational spaces within the same area. This will create vibrant neighbourhoods, reduce commuting distances, and promote walkability and community interaction.
Promotion of self-redevelopment	In self-redevelopment projects, the residents of a housing society collectively undertake the responsibility of financing, planning, and executing the redevelopment process.
Smart City Technologies	Integrate smart city technologies to enhance urban services and improve efficiency. Implement intelligent transportation systems, digital infrastructure, and data-driven urban management for better resource utilisation and quality of life.
Transit-Oriented Development	Focus on transit-oriented development around major transport hubs and metro stations. Create pedestrian-friendly environments, provide last-mile connectivity, and encourage mixed-use developments to reduce reliance on private vehicles.
Waterfront Development	Utilise the potential of waterfront areas for recreation, tourism, and economic activities. Develop promenades, marinas, and waterfront parks to enhance the coastal charm of the MMR and create vibrant public spaces.

Revitalisation Suggestions	Description
Affordable Housing	Implement more affordable housing projects and schemes to address the housing needs of different income groups. Encourage public-private partnerships and innovative financing models to make affordable housing accessible to a larger population.
Integrated Infrastructure	Enhance infrastructure integration by connecting different modes of transportation, such as metro, suburban rail, and bus services. Improve last-mile connectivity, reduce travel time, and ensure seamless movement across the MMR.
Tourist Infrastructure	Improve tourist infrastructure by upgrading amenities, signage, and information centres. Develop tourist circuits and promote guided tours that showcase the MMR's diverse cultural, historical, and natural attractions.

Evaluating and exploring the alternative approaches to urban planning and Development

The FSI policy in Mumbai has been a subject of heated discussions and debates. While opinions on the FSI policy may vary, let's look at some of the pros and cons:

Pros	Cons
1. Increased vertical development: The FSI policy allows for increased vertical development, enabling the construction of taller buildings. This helps accommodate the growing population and optimises land utilisation.	1. Strain on infrastructure: Increased vertical development without adequate planning can strain existing amenities such as roads, water supply, and sewage systems.

Pros	Cons
2. Maximising land potential: The FSI policy allows owners to maximise the potential of their land by utilising the available FSI and constructing additional floors. This can lead to efficient land use and increased housing supply.	2. Congestion and overcrowding: The increased density resulting from higher FSI can contribute to congestion and overcrowding in certain areas, impacting the quality of life and public spaces.
3. Incentive for redevelopment: The FSI policy incentivises redevelopment by allowing property owners to construct additional floors or sell additional FSI rights. This encourages the redevelopment of older buildings and promotes urban revitalisation.	3. Loss of architectural character: High FSI can result in the demolition of heritage buildings and the loss of the city's architectural character as older structures are replaced with taller, more modern buildings.
4. Affordable housing opportunities: By allowing for increased construction and housing supply, the FSI policy can create opportunities to develop affordable housing units, addressing the housing affordability challenge in Mumbai.	4. Impact on sunlight and ventilation: Higher FSI can lead to reduced access to sunlight and ventilation for existing buildings and surrounding areas, affecting the quality of life for residents.
5. Revenue generation: The FSI policy provides opportunities for the government to generate revenue by selling additional FSI rights, which can be used for infrastructure development, public amenities, and urban improvement projects.	5. Impact on infrastructure capacity: Higher FSI can strain the existing infrastructure capacity, including transportation networks, schools, healthcare facilities, and public services, necessitating additional investments to meet the increased demand.

Alternatives to the FSI policy:

Several alternatives to the Floor Space Index (FSI) policy can be considered for urban development. Here are some common alternatives:

Plot Ratio: Plot ratio, also known as plot coverage or plot intensity, is a policy that determines the maximum allowable built-up area in relation to the total area of the plot. It sets a limit on the plot percentage that can be developed, irrespective of the height of the building. Plot ratio-based regulations promote controlled and balanced development, ensuring that the built-up area is proportional to the available land area.

Building Height Restrictions: Instead of focusing on floor area, building height restrictions establish limits on the maximum height of structures. This approach helps maintain the visual character of a city or specific areas, preserves views and ensures compatibility with the surrounding built environment. By regulating height, cities can control density and promote appropriate development following the urban context.

Form-Based Codes: Form-based codes emphasise buildings' physical form and design rather than relying solely on floor area or density. These codes focus on factors such as building setbacks, street frontages, building heights, and architectural style to shape the character of an area. Form-based codes create vibrant and pedestrian-friendly neighbourhoods by promoting a cohesive and visually appealing urban environment.

Performance-Based Zoning: Performance-based zoning sets specific performance criteria rather than rigid numerical regulations. This approach focuses on achieving desired outcomes such as environmental sustainability, energy efficiency, and quality of life. Developers have flexibility in meeting these performance standards, encouraging innovative design solutions while ensuring compliance with overall urban goals.

Development Impact Fees: Development impact fees are charges imposed on developers to mitigate the impacts of new development on public infrastructure and services. The fees collected are used to fund improvements in transportation, utilities, schools, parks, and other essential amenities. By linking development with infrastructure funding, impact fees help ensure that growth costs are shared and that the necessary infrastructure is in place to support new developments.

Design Guidelines and Standards: Design guidelines and standards provide specific criteria and requirements for the design and aesthetics of buildings and developments. These guidelines focus on building materials, architectural style, landscaping, and site design. By establishing design expectations, cities can ensure that new developments contribute to the overall character and quality of the urban environment.

It is crucial to understand that the effectiveness of these options can vary according to the specific needs, objectives, and priorities of a city or region. To tackle the unique challenges and opportunities of each urban area, it is imperative to employ a combination of these options or tailor the approach accordingly.

City	Alternative Approach Implemented
Vancouver, Canada	Form-Based Code (Vancouver Building By-law)
Portland, Oregon, United States	Transit-Oriented Development Strategy, Design Guidelines
Tokyo, Japan	Plot Ratio Regulations, Building Height Restrictions
Curitiba, Brazil	Performance-Based Zoning, Sustainable Development Strategies
Portland, Maine, United States	Development Impact Fee System

These alternative approaches have been adopted in these cities to shape urban development, promote sustainability, enhance design quality, improve transportation, and manage growth. Each city's approach is tailored to its specific context, goals, and challenges, demonstrating the diversity of urban planning and development strategies.

Conclusion

In conclusion, revitalising the Mumbai Metropolitan Region (MMR) is an urgent and complex task requiring various stakeholders' multifaceted approach and collaborative efforts. This chapter has explored several key aspects and strategies for revitalisation, highlighting the region's challenges and presenting potential solutions.

First and foremost, addressing the issues of infrastructure, transportation, and housing is crucial for the sustainable development of the MMR. Upgrading and expanding the existing infrastructure network, investing in efficient public transportation systems, and implementing innovative housing solutions can help alleviate congestion, improve connectivity, and provide affordable housing options for the growing population.

Furthermore, focusing on sustainable and inclusive urban planning is paramount. Integrating green spaces, promoting mixed-use developments, and adopting smart city technologies can create liveable and environmentally friendly neighbourhoods. Emphasising transit-oriented development, preserving heritage sites, and enhancing public spaces can contribute to a vibrant and culturally rich urban fabric.

Additionally, economic diversification and promoting entrepreneurship are vital for revitalising the MMR. Encouraging innovation, supporting small and medium enterprises, and attracting investments in sectors beyond traditional industries can create employment opportunities, foster economic growth, and reduce dependency on specific sectors.

Moreover, active citizen participation and engagement should be at the core of revitalisation efforts. Inclusive decision-making processes, community involvement, and partnerships with non-governmental organisations can ensure that the aspirations and needs of the residents are considered. Empowering communities and fostering a sense of ownership can lead to more sustainable and inclusive development outcomes.

The MMR is a long-term endeavour that requires sustained commitment, adequate resources, and effective governance. Collaboration between government bodies, private sector entities, community organisations, and citizens is essential for implementing comprehensive and integrated strategies.

Revising the Mumbai Metropolitan Region can create a more inclusive, sustainable, and prosperous urban environment for its residents. Through infrastructure development, sustainable urban planning, economic diversification, and citizen participation, the MMR can overcome its challenges and emerge as a model metropolis that embodies the principles of liveability, resilience, and social well-being. The success of these revitalisation efforts will depend on the collective determination and collaborative actions of all stakeholders involved.

Chapter 14

FSI: A Boon or Bane

Introduction

So far in this book, we have discussed how land was used over the centuries, what exactly FSI is, different types of FSI, FSI rules and regulations in residential, commercial and industrial areas. Now we are here to answer a very important question; is a higher FSI necessarily even better?

Let's look at the pros of higher FSI first:

1. Efficient land use: Higher FSI allows for more efficient utilisation of limited land resources in urban areas. Allowing taller buildings or more floors enables a greater number of residential, commercial, or mixed-use spaces to be developed on the same plot of land.

2. Increased housing supply: Higher FSI can help address housing shortages in densely populated areas. Maximising the use of available land facilitates the construction of more residential units, contributing to increased housing supply. This is particularly beneficial in urban areas with high population density and limited space for expansion.

3. Reduced urban sprawl: By encouraging vertical development, higher FSI can help combat urban sprawl. Instead of spreading outward into suburban areas, cities can grow vertically, reducing the need to extend infrastructure and services over larger areas. This can lead to more sustainable urban development patterns.

4. Enhanced transportation efficiency: Concentrating development in urban centres through higher FSI can

improve transportation efficiency. The higher population density in these areas supports the development of public transportation systems. It reduces commuting distances, promoting sustainable modes of transport and reducing congestion and pollution.

5. Economic benefits: Higher FSI can generate economic benefits for developers and local governments. Developers can maximise their returns on investment by constructing more floors or additional buildings on a given land parcel. Local governments can generate increased property tax revenue and benefit from higher economic activity associated with denser development.

6. Infrastructure optimisation: Higher FSI often prompts or requires developers to invest in necessary infrastructure improvements. When higher-density projects are developed, there is an increased incentive for developers and local governments to upgrade utilities, transportation networks, and community facilities to accommodate the larger population, resulting in overall infrastructure optimisation.

7. Vibrant urban environment: Higher FSI can contribute to creating vibrant and dynamic urban environments. Concentrated development leads to a mix of residential, commercial, and cultural spaces nearby, fostering walkability, diversity, and a sense of community. It can also support the establishment of amenities such as parks, schools, and recreational facilities.

8. Reduction in cost for the customer: Higher FSI allows developers to allow projects to sell for cheaper, as they can construct more flats in the same space. This is vital for cities like Mumbai, where land prices have skyrocketed.

These are some very good arguments about why a higher FSI is better. But there are a few cons as well.

1. Overcrowding and congestion: Higher FSI can lead to overcrowding and increased population density in an area. This can result in congestion on roads and public

transportation systems, overcrowded public spaces, and strained infrastructure and services, such as water supply, schools, and sewage systems. More infrastructure to support the increased population can positively impact the residents' quality of life.

2. Reduced sunlight and ventilation: With increased building heights and reduced setbacks between structures, higher FSI can lead to a lack of sunlight and limited ventilation. Tall buildings can cast shadows over neighbouring properties, reducing natural light availability and potentially compromising the livability of surrounding areas. Insufficient airflow and limited access to fresh air can also affect residents' overall comfort and well-being.

3. The strain on utilities and services: Higher FSI can significantly strain existing utilities and public services. The increased demand for electricity, water, and other resources may surpass the capacity of the current infrastructure, leading to service disruptions, inefficiencies, or increased costs. Upgrading or expanding infrastructure to accommodate the higher demand can be costly and time-consuming.

4. Loss of green spaces: As FSI increases, the available land for open spaces, parks, and recreational areas decreases. This can result in losing green spaces within urban environments, essential for promoting physical and mental well-being, providing recreational opportunities, and mitigating the heat island effect. The lack of access to nature and open spaces can negatively impact the residents' quality of life.

5. Impact on heritage and aesthetics: Higher FSI can negatively impact an area's aesthetic appeal and cultural heritage. It may result in the overshadowing or dwarfing historical or landmark structures, compromising their visual prominence and cultural significance. The neighbourhood or cityscape's overall architectural character and harmony can also be affected if new developments do not align with existing design patterns or building styles.

6. Risk of inadequate planning: Increasing FSI without appropriate urban planning and regulations can result in haphazard development and inadequate public amenities and services provision. There needs to be more consideration of traffic management, parking, waste management, and emergency services to avoid increased urban problems and decreased liveability.

Conclusion

As we can see, the answer is somewhere in between. Sure, higher FSI brings many benefits economically and allows the most efficient use of land. However, it comes at the cost of quality of life for everyone, as more people have to live in the same square footage area than before.

In cities like Mumbai, where the population is increasing rapidly for various reasons, new schools, hospitals, and recreational areas aren't being built because land prices are exorbitantly high, and there needs to be more space in general. This means that even though the population is increasing, the social infrastructure cannot keep up.

The key lies in proper town planning. The advantages of higher FSI can only be taken if the rest of the infrastructure can keep up with it. There needs to be a balance between tall buildings, decongested roads, open green spaces, and the feeling of just an overall lack of personal space.

Areas that may not be efficiently developed need to be focused on. Slums need to be redeveloped to improve the standard of living of the slum dwellers, as well as decongest the suburbs. And lastly, the architectural history of a city needs to be preserved.

www.ingramcontent.com/pod-product-compliance
Lightning Source LLC
Chambersburg PA
CBHW021206130726
47988CB00002B/530